It's All Ab
The $Money, Honey!®

REAL TALK ABOUT BUILDING WEALTH

Victoria L. Woods

The Financial Diva & Chief Investment Advisor

SPARK Publications
Charlotte, North Carolina

It's All About The $Money, Honey!®
Real Talk about Building Wealth
By Victoria L. Woods

Designed, produced, and published by SPARK Publications
SPARKpublications.com
Charlotte, North Carolina

Cover and author photography by Joe Stewart Photography

Printed in the United States of America

First edition, paperback, October 2007, ISBN 978-0-9779689-0-9

Second edition, format, April 2022, ISBN: 978-1-953555-17-5

Library of Congress Control Number: 2021918033

Dedication

*To my husband, Larry Woods, who has been
my constant support, encouragement, and
inspiration for over thirty-eight years. He gives
me my wings to fly. The best investment I
have ever or will ever make: my marriage.*

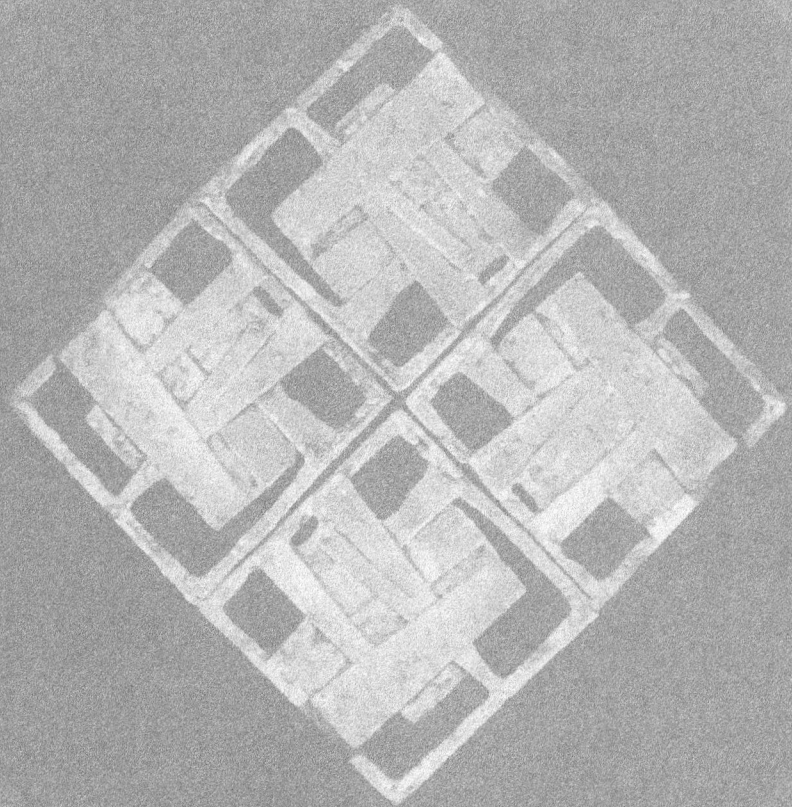

Foreword

The Financial Diva, Victoria Woods, and
Second Edition of her breakout book,
It's All About The $Money, Honey!®

Victoria Woods started her first business at age eleven and went on to become a self-made, award-winning entrepreneur, radio talk show host, and motivational speaker with over twenty years' experience as a financial advisor. Ask the listeners who trust her, the business leaders who admire her, and all the folks in Oklahoma who know her. Victoria is absolutely unstoppable as an advisor to mid-tier millionaires. She wrote "It's All About The $Money, Honey!®" as a calling card for her highly successful management firm, ChappelWood Financial Services.

As far as background, Victoria has established her authority and holds exceptional credentials. She participated in the President's Small Business Summit and was named "Woman of the Year" by the Governor of Oklahoma in 2001. As the mastermind behind creating the Financial District of Oklahoma, she received the 2002 "Innovator of the Year" award from *The Journal Record* of Oklahoma City, the "Best of the Best" award from the National Association of Women Business Owners, and Wealth Management Award in Athens, Greece. Above all, Victoria is an advocate for educating children about the importance of financial planning at a very early age. She lobbied for legislation to establish mandatory financial literacy classes for grades seven through twelve, starting with the 2008/2009 school year. Finally, you should know Victoria is dedicated to doing good, as a portion of her royalties will go to multiple charities. She supports charities such as the YWCA for Domestic Violence Services, Allied Arts of Oklahoma City, veterans and police officers and their families.

It has been proven that money is one of the highest stressors that women face. Too often, they turn over control of their money to their spouses, significant others, employers or ignore it all together… in essence putting their heads in the sand related to understanding their financial position. And yet, it is also a known fact that when women take action, like learning to save and invest, their confidence grows exponentially, and they are more likely to meet their goals.

Victoria has a disarming and really approachable way of advising her clients and her readers on navigating the complexities of financial planning. That's why she is so appealing. She literally started from the ground up and now wants to advise you on your finances and how to grow, preserve, and distribute your assets.

In this book, Victoria shares strategies and tools that will help you take control of your financial life and create the success you deserve!

To your financial success!

Sharon Lechter, CGMA
CEO and Founder of Pay Your Family First
www.sharonlechter.com
Global Financial Literacy Expert, 5 times NYTs Bestselling Author

"

It has been proven that money is one of the highest stressors that women face. Too often they turn over control of their money to their spouses, significant others, employers or ignore it all together... in essence putting their heads in the sand related to understanding their financial position.

"

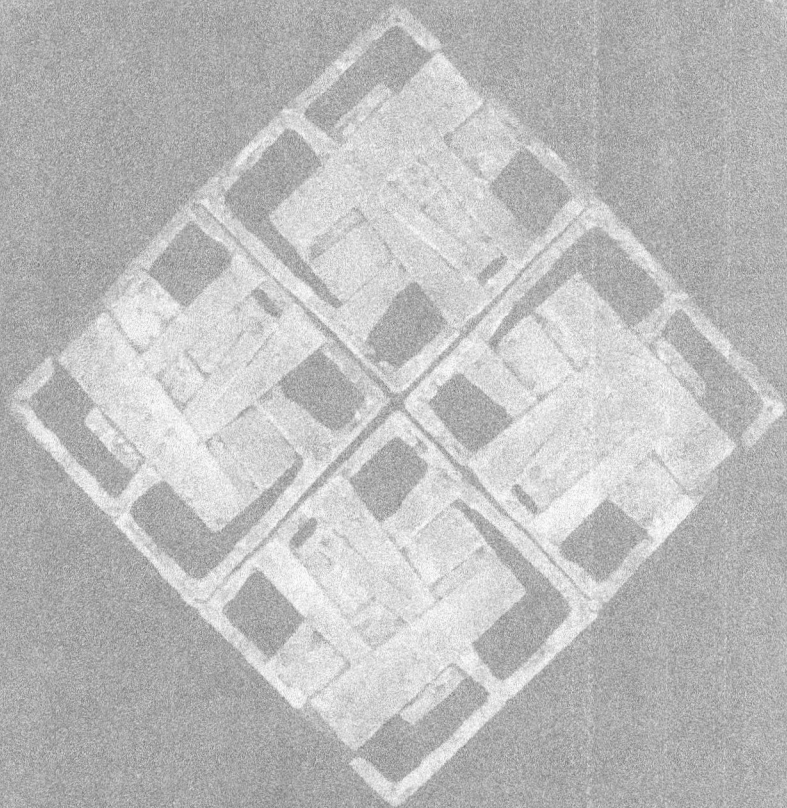

The Diva's Favorite Poem

[1]*It Is Rewarding*

It is rewarding to find someone who you like,
but it is essential to like yourself.

It is quickening to recognize that someone is a good and decent
human being, but it is indispensable to view yourself as acceptable.

It is a delight to discover people who are worthy of
respect and admiration and love, but it is vital to
believe yourself deserving of these things.

For you cannot live in someone else. You cannot find
yourself in someone else. Of all the people you will know
in a lifetime, you are the only one you will never leave nor
lose. To the question of your life, you are the only answer.
To the problems of your life, you are the only solution.

Jo Coudert, *Advice from a Failure*

---

1   Jo Coudert, *Advice from a Failure* (iUniverse 2007).

Table of Contents

List of Tables
& Illustrations

Acknowledgments

For Those Who Encourage, Support, and Inspire Me

To Chuck and Gayle Hodges of Palm Springs, California: this book would not be possible without your kind offer of the use of your cabin in Big Bear, California. My husband thought I was the most generous person he'd ever met—and then he met Chuck!

To my staff at ChappelWood Financial Services: thank you for taking such good care of the office and our clients while I put my thoughts, experience, and opinions on paper for the world to see. You gave me great confidence and allowed me to focus.

And to Heather Rice: without you this could not have been possible. You found us a location to research and to broadcast my radio show. You kept me on track, didn't allow me to make too many friends except for Lucy and Brian Cannon from San Diego, the ladies in the Christmas store, the guy in the card store, and of course Chris and Steve. And thank you for allowing me to take a break and watch *Dancing with The Stars*! You were the perfect companion for this project.

My thanks also to my clients, my radio listeners, friends, family, and business associates—especially Steve Gust. You are my constant source of encouragement, support, and inspiration.

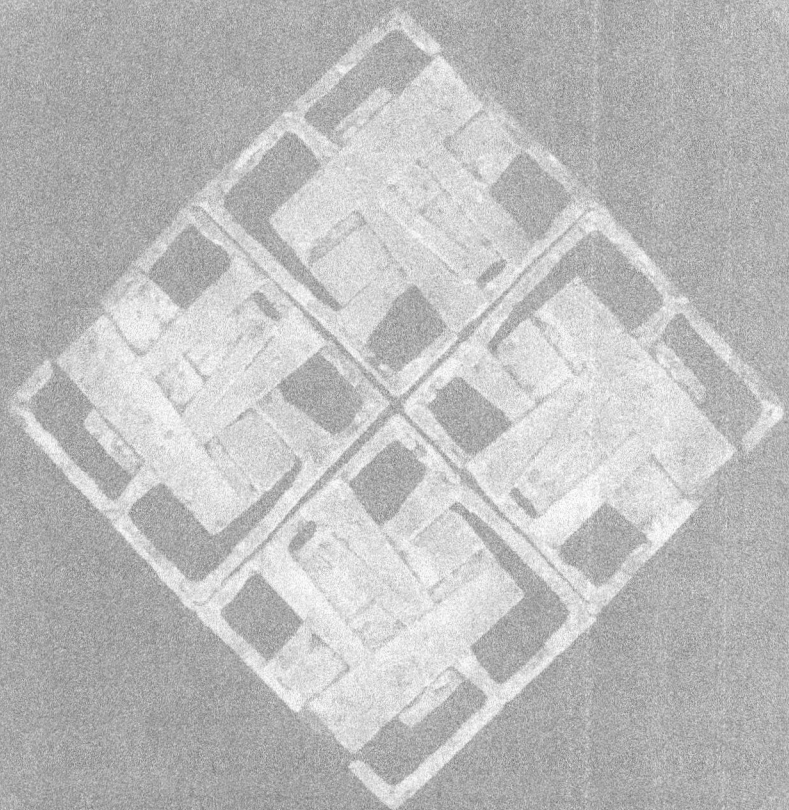

Introduction

We are all provided tools, resources, and
opportunities; it's how we execute.
—Diva

Welcome to my book, and please allow me to wish you a hearty congratulations! This little journey you and I are about to go on may be one of the most important you'll ever make. After we're done, you may have thousands, hundreds of thousands, or even millions of reasons to be very grateful you invested the time reading this. After you've profited from this venture, tell your friends and relatives. Allow them to benefit too!

I'm here to share some of my real-life experiences as well as stories from my clients and radio listeners. You may be one of my clients or listeners, or maybe you've just heard one of my speeches[2] such as "Where Fun Meets Finance!" or this book may be our first contact. However we made contact, together we can learn to make your money future much brighter!

The lessons in this book, when followed, will teach you how to create wealth. You'll learn how debt is working against you and how to find the right financial advisor for your needs. You'll also gain some practical knowledge on what every investor needs to know—

---

2 Guest speaking appearances at FinancialDiva.com

including that big investment, real estate. We'll cover the successes and, yes, even the mistakes. Life's lessons are never all good, and you may get a chuckle at someone else's experience—mine!

Don't expect to be reading a college economics textbook, although I have no doubt many professors and students would gain a lot of knowledge from what's taught here. We will be diving headfirst into real life with practical principles and the right steps. Don't expect any theory. There are plenty of books on those subjects. This narrative is from someone who has been there and done it.

This book is for those wanting to create wealth by walking with someone who has been through the minefield and made it to the other side with her integrity intact, alive, healthy, happy, and yes, with much, much more than when she started.

I'm excited to get started. Before we begin, let's look at the need for a financial advisor. After all, you may be thinking, "It is my money. I earned it; why do I need help managing it?" The reality is that you are facing some pretty challenging economic decisions—both long and short term.

Can you honestly say you're completely prepared? Do you have all the answers? Do you even have all the questions? Allow me to illustrate. Could you repair your car on your own? If you're like most of us, the answer is "no." You'd need someone with expertise. Compared to a car, the stakes are much, much higher with your financial future. Is your portfolio in need of some major repair? You're not alone. The right advisor can have a huge impact and make the difference between wealth and security or some poor money decisions. The right advisor could mean the difference between an Ivy League education for your children or a community college degree. You and your family deserve a stress-free financial future. I'll show you how to make that happen.

Three Reasons for Money Management

First, we will continue to see a huge transfer of money from a generation who were savers to a generation who are consumers and spenders. A study[3] was done by Paul G. Schervish and John J. Havens that predicted that over the fifty-five year period from 1998 to 2052, a minimum of $41 trillion will pass from the generation of savers to the generation of spenders. From my perspective of over thirty years as a financial advisor, this is a perfect recipe for a disaster! The majority of the generation receiving these funds need a compass. They don't have the experience or knowledge to manage their inheritance. Believe me, it is a minefield out there.

Second, not everyone is fortunate enough to have parents, teachers, aunts, uncles, grandparents, or mentors to teach them money management skills. All one has to do is look at the misuse of credit cards. This alone proves my point.

Third, there is a growing group of Americans transforming society. You may be a mid-tier millionaire. If you are, you are one of the fastest-growing economic segments in the nation. Your numbers, some estimate, will swell to $11 million. Your wealth ranges from $5 million to $30 million.

The problem with mid-tier millionaires is, when they reach a certain level, they tend to protect their income. Money needs to be put to work with solid investments. Why? Because you want to reach the goal all of us have—financial independence. Being financially independent means that you own 100 percent of your time. Don't you want that? Who doesn't?

I want to share my forty years of real-life financial experience to better help you with your money skills, so you don't have to go through it alone.

Financial Advisors: Getting You Through the Money Minefield

Educate and Inform

An informed investor is a better investor. Period. Don't make the mistake of sticking your head in the sand when you hear words like

_____
3   John J. Havens, and Paul G. Schervish, "Millionaires and the Millennium: New Estimates of the Forthcoming Wealth Transfer and the Prospects for a Golden Age of Philanthropy." (Boston College Social Welfare Research Institute, 1999)

401(k), investments, and compounded interest. Learning about all your money opportunities can be fun and exciting. Unfortunately, many people panic at the thought of absorbing so much information, and they learn their financial lessons the hard way. Do you know everything about stocks, bonds, mutual funds, 401(k)s, IRAs, annuities, wills, trusts, or taxes? Do you understand the lexicon? If not, it may cost you, your heirs, and your legacy dearly.

Provide Organization

When prospective clients come to my office, they have a multitude of accounts and are frustrated as well as confused. I visualize all their different accounts as colored balloons rising over their heads. My goal is to clarify, organize, and simplify their lives and put all the red balloons, blue balloons, and yellow balloons together—and that's just the beginning.

Provide an Action Plan

At ChappelWood Financial Services, which I founded in Edmond, Oklahoma, in 1988, everyone—including client, advisor, implementation manager, Certified Public Accountant (CPA), tax attorney, real estate specialist, long-term care specialist, and trust attorney—is clear regarding what we have agreed to do and who's responsible for the implementation and the date it is to be accomplished. How can you possibly have confidence if you don't have a plan, process, and steps to accomplish your plan?

My Own Minefield

Some of you may like what you've read so far. Great! You may be wondering, however, why *I* am the Diva of giving financial advice and, more importantly, what I can teach you.

Since founding ChappelWood, I've helped people achieve their money dreams. My experience in sales, sales training, and business management, however, started long before that. You might say my trip through the minefield began at age twelve when I began babysitting to earn lunch money. At times, I would babysit six children at once. I discovered a long time ago to look for work opportunities because work equaled money.

By age fifteen, I got permission for my first "real" job at Montgomery Ward. At one time, I worked three jobs to go to college—one full time and two part-time. The hard work paid off at Ward's with promotions, and while in my early twenties, I became their youngest buyer. While with Ward's regional buying office in the Overland Park area of Kansas City, I took some additional university courses on my own, including accounting and personal finance. Those classes gave me a good, solid foundation for a career in money management.

When I was growing up, my family didn't have savings. Sometimes, all we had to eat were ketchup and onion sandwiches because all we could grow behind our garage was potatoes, onions, and strawberries. Getting into financial services gave me the opportunity to educate myself on saving and investing.

I entered the field in the 1980s and quickly realized financial services would allow me to help people by showing them how to save money for retirement and leave a social legacy. I'll talk a little more about this later.

When my husband, Larry, and I moved to Oklahoma in 1988, I received some very sound advice from Steve Owens, a property and casualty agency owner in Norman. He is also college football's 1969 Heisman Trophy winner for the University of Oklahoma Sooners.

"I want you to understand that we treat our clients as our friends because that's who they are," he told me.

I'll never forget that. It didn't matter whether they were friends and clients or clients and friends because that was his attitude—it's been mine as well.

Why "The Financial Diva"?

Years ago, I was doing a talk radio segment with Clear Channel Communications. Right before a commercial break, the host urged listeners to stay tuned for more advice from "The Financial Diva," Victoria Woods. To be honest, I didn't give it a second thought at the time. I should have. Starting the next day and several months following, I was inundated by the new role as the "Financial Diva." At first, I didn't completely embrace this unique title; however, I later realized it gave me an identity that connected with my listeners and clients. This name has made it easier for me to share my knowledge on money matters. In the process, I've been able to help many, many people.

I now have my own radio program where the Financial Diva regularly gives sound money advice. The Financial Diva has taken on a life of its own now. To learn more, visit my web page at FinancialDiva.com. This career has helped me make friends and faithful clients across the country. I am always fascinated by their businesses and what I can do to help them grow. This career has also helped me on my road to success. I have operated three successful small businesses and founded the eighty-four-acre Financial District of Oklahoma. Oklahoma's governor and the president of the United States have honored me, and I have built a sound financial services business.

My hope and my desire are that when you take the time to read some of my stories, they inspire, encourage, and support your decisions and financial goals. This book will show you that if a girl who had no lunch money and grew up on ketchup and onion sandwiches can succeed, you can too. I truly believe this with all my heart. I know where I came from, and I'll never forget it, and I value every person I've met and all my experiences in life that molded me into who I am today.

Let's make you one of the thousands I've been able to help! Enjoy! Let's get started, and please turn the page!

"

My hope and my desire are that
when you take the time to read
some of my stories, they inspire,
encourage, and support your
decisions and financial goals.

"

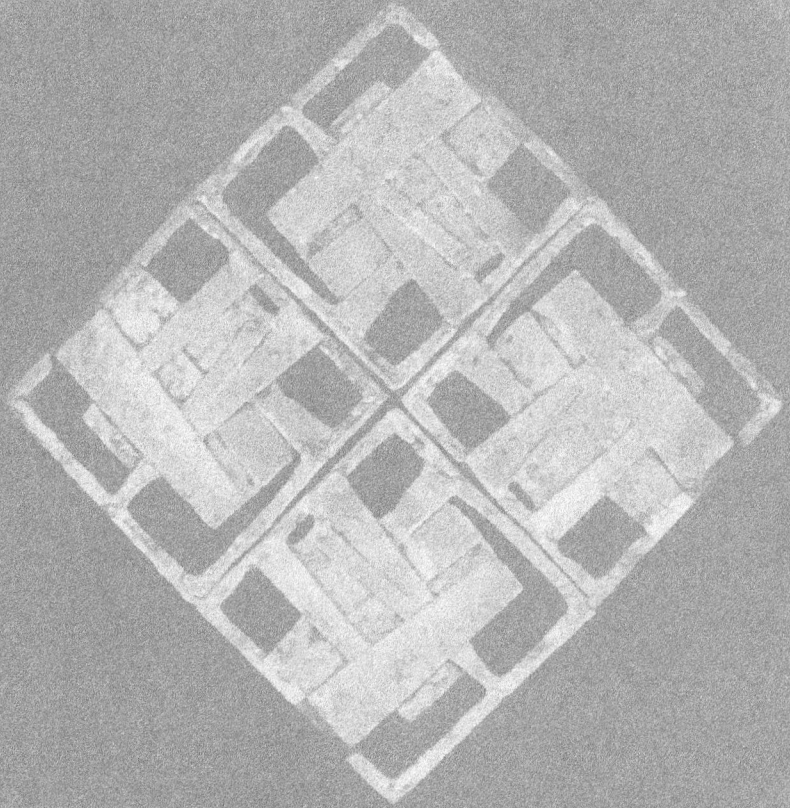

CHAPTER 1

The Diva Speaks

Don't take advice from broke people.
—Diva

O n the surface, to say "don't take advice from broke people" may seem blunt. Allow me to explain. The saying applies to money matters while also applying to spiritual and physical journeys.

Let's say you were trying to lose twenty pounds. Would you seek advice from someone who had struggled with weight all of their life? Or would you consult with someone who had a weight problem, took off the excess pounds, and kept them off?

If you were having spiritual difficulties, would it make sense to ask someone who's never opened a Bible, has no personal daily relationship with our Creator, or has never seen the inside of a church or temple?

When it comes to money, do you solicit advice from someone who has filed bankruptcy or from your unemployed brother-in-law who's got a "hot tip?" Absolutely not!

In all three matters, you go to the people with the expertise, who've overcome adversity, and are successful. For this reason, I know I can help you make the right money decisions.

What Do I Know about Money?

As I like to say, "It's *All* About The $Money, Honey!®" You don't have to have it to be happy, just like you don't need a bed to sleep. I've always been happy, even without money. Do I like having money rather than not having it? Absolutely! Anyone who tells you otherwise is not telling the truth. I admit that I'm one of those advisors who encourages travel, furs, diamonds, boats, cars, and planes as well as second, third, and fourth homes.

Think of all the things you could do when you have a million dollars—that's not a lot of money in the twenty-first century. OK, I can hear you screaming now: "What did you say? One million dollars would change my life, Victoria!"

Yes, it would. It's my hope that it would also change the lives of people around you—friends, family, church, charities, and community. It's our responsibility to enrich others through our talents and gifts. Even with money, there's truth to the saying, "Of those who are given much, much is expected."

Everything is relative—especially where money is concerned. Having only $1 million might seem like poverty to some. Let me illustrate with a story. Do you remember pay phones?

The cell-phone generation might not appreciate this; however, at one time in the not-too-distant past, pay phones were all we had when we were out in public and needed to communicate. In the 1960s, a pay phone would give that magic dial tone—provided you dropped a dime or two nickels down the coin chute.

Imagine having a vital call to make and you only have a nickel. Finding another nickel would be as important as having a stack of $100 bills because absolutely nothing else would do. In other words, a nickel may seem like a small coin; however, that emergency phone call could mean the difference between life and death.

Suppose you were going to start your dream business and needed a cool $1 million to make it a reality. Unfortunately, you could only get a loan for $800,000. How important would that $200,000 be?

It would mean everything in the world! A nickel or $200,000 can make a huge difference—it's all relative.

Having $1 million would make some feel like the richest man or woman in the world. On the other hand, if Oprah had only $1 million, she'd feel like a pauper—broke and starving. So the meaning of how much money we have is relative. What amounts to "a lot" is different for everyone.

Again, you don't have to have money to be happy. Years ago, my home was a humble Texas apartment. On occasion, I would have my own little "Lone Star roundup." I wasn't driving cattle; I was gathering pennies and herding them into those little paper rolls. Why would I take the time to mess with Abe Lincoln? Simple: I needed gas money to make it to work. In those days I had little to no money, yet I was happy. Today, I have plenty of money, and guess what—I'm still happy!

Understanding Universal Laws

For me it's truly been a journey, and I've enjoyed every bit of it. What I learned is that there are basic principles of how to manage money and how money works in a person's life. It doesn't matter who you are or what you do, these principles are the same for all of us.

Let's have some real fun. Open your mind and participate in an exercise with me. Imagine yourself at a swimming pool on a bright, sunny day. Remember when you were a kid, and all your friends and you lined up for the high dive on those bright 100-degree days? If it helps, close your eyes. You can hear the splashing of the water and smell the Coppertone, Hawaiian Tropic, and baby oil. There's a twist this time. You're on the high-diving board, and right up there with you are the president of the United States and Oprah.

When the president, Oprah, and you take turns stepping off the high dive, where are all of you going? Down. Yes, straight down.

This is a law of the universe. Your social status doesn't matter. Your gender, skin color, and bank account don't figure into the equation either. Darlin', all three of you are going down. Nothing any of you do can change that. Let's also hope someone remembered to put water in the pool or you will learn a less pleasant lesson—the law of gravity.

The point? If you don't understand universal laws, you'll never understand the power and concept of managing money and how it works in your life. If you don't have money working for you in your life, or enough of it, then it's time you change your thinking. Before going further, reread this exercise and ponder it. If necessary, call a friend to explain it to you, or try jumping off a diving board. In an emergency, call 1-888-838-DIVA, and I will illustrate it further. This is important!

If you don't grasp this, you'll continue to struggle. If you're struggling, take a long, hard look at what you're doing with your money now. As television sage Dr. Phil might ask, "How's that working for ya?" Wouldn't you rather have money flow to you easily and effortlessly? Who wouldn't?

Money's Universal Laws

Like the universal laws of nature, the basic principles or universal laws of money are the same for everyone. Applying these basic laws will work. Take the Diva's word for it. I started with less than nothing. One of my business associates, Edward Lee, Esq. of Edmond, Oklahoma, knows my story and has been quoted as saying, "I have been an attorney for twenty years, and Victoria Woods has done more with less than anyone I know."

In America, we have it backwards. Let's face it: we want to reap before we sow (entitlement), get before we give (charity), and spend before we earn (borrowing). Paul Kasriel, director of economic research of Northern Trust, noted in the *Oklahoman* (August 15, 2007) that from 1929 to 2000, there were only seven years in which American households spent more than they earned after taxes. In contrast, every year from 2001 to 2006, Americans spent more than they earned! Where did this nonsense come from? Successful people, or wealth creators, do just the opposite. They sow before they reap, give before they get, and earn before they spend.

I know what you're thinking: "Victoria, I don't have enough money to pay my bills much less give any of it away!"

You need to read the diving-board exercise once again and ponder universal laws—and please, get Dr. Joseph Murphy's *The Power of Your Subconscious Mind*. It's a must-read for everyone who can read. You *must* change your thinking! If the formula works for successful people, what makes you think you can do things differently?

To repeat: give first, save second, and spend third because when you give, that gift will come back to you many times over. There are some secrets to successful giving. When you think you're giving your last dime, you bless that money and give joyfully without fear. My dear friend, Gayle, reminds me of this.

I know this from personal experience. Once, I strayed from the financial formula and purchased my first office building. It was a bank building, and it was a big investment for me. At that same time, a young man named Sean Vanlandingham asked me to give to a church mission trip. Regretfully, I politely declined because I believed I couldn't afford it at the time. I agonized over whether I had done the right thing.

The next time Sean asked me to donate, I wrote him a check even though I didn't know how I was going to make payroll and meet all my other financial obligations. I was in for a surprise. When the time came, I had more than enough to take care of my business needs. The reason, I believe, is simple: what you "think" about or believe is what you create. I always believe I will have more than enough even if it doesn't appear to be the case on paper or in my bank account.

What I gained most from making this donation became apparent when Sean returned from the trip and invited several of us to his parents' home to share his experience. I was in awe of what these young people had accomplished and what Sean had gained from his mission work. His experience will benefit him and countless others—he'll be an inspiration to others for the rest of his life. What a great investment! Again, you must give first.

Second, you must pay yourself first. It may surprise you to know that according to Dun & Bradstreet, the average American spends $1.20 for every dollar earned. It doesn't take a great number cruncher to know that this will put you in the poor house. It may seem like common sense, yet many people need to be reminded of a simple fact: it's impossible to create wealth by spending more than you earn! So don't live above your means. It probably wouldn't hurt to reread the last few sentences; let the words sink in and share them with those you love as well.

Dare to Be Different!

Do you want to be average? If so, just keep doing what you're doing. The smart thing to do, though, is to spend only after you have given and saved. What does that mean? It means that when you aren't creating wealth in your life, *you* must make some changes. Do it now! Maybe that means the dreaded "B" word—budget! If you're spending more than you earn, *you*, my friend, are in debt and cannot create wealth by being in debt—especially credit card debt.

You must compile a net worth statement. It's a very sexy thing to have. The more zeros in your liabilities, the sexier you are. You also must create a budget. You can make it simple or complex. A budget will let you know in black and white your financial condition. It may be good or ugly. At the least, you will know where you are—you can't make positive changes until you know this information. And you must set goals and write them out—if you don't write them down it doesn't count. I'm providing a starting place by including the necessary forms at the end of this chapter including a Net Worth form, a Simple Budget form, and a Financial Goal worksheet. *(To print out, go to chappelwood.com).*

People spend more time planning their annual vacations or what movie to see than they spend putting together an effective, long-range road map for financial success. I spent two weeks in the Mediterranean and had a great time. This fourteen-day excursion took months of solid planning. A retirement can last thirty years or more. Shouldn't retirement be an exciting and wonderful stage of life and demand at least the same kind of planning and thought?

There's a phrase you've heard before, and in your heart, you know it's true: "You do not create wealth by accident." A friend of mine, Phyllis Busch, often says, "Life is full of choices." Whether you choose to believe it or not, the fact that it's true doesn't change. Look how you're struggling now. Are you frustrated? I think I just heard Dr. Phil again: "How's that working for ya?" If you want to continue to struggle, keep on doing what you're doing. I've chosen to follow a path to creating wealth and have been applying these principles to my life since I was twenty-three. My path of wealth creation leads to great expectations. My husband jokes about me loving to go to the mailbox. The reason I love the trip to the mailbox is because I expect unexpected checks. Just recently, I received an unexpected check for $1,986.13 because I expected unexpected money to come in—always have, always will.

I'm human—at times I get off track; however, having learned these basic financial principles, I always know how to make my life easier by getting back on track and applying these principles properly. When you don't have a plan, you're planning to fail. The good news is that you can take charge of your money and life right now.

THE DIVA'S ADVICE

1. Don't take advice from broke people. This is the best advice I can give you. This applies not only to your financial life, but to your physical and spiritual life as well.
2. Money by itself won't make you happy.
3. Money is relative. Remember the payphone illustration.
4. Money operates with its own universal laws. When you think about debt, you'll create debt. When you think about creating wealth, you'll start creating wealth; simply attracting it like a magnet. Sadly, most people never take the time to learn the universal laws of money. Even sadder is that some who learn them never apply them.
5. You sow to reap.
6. You give to get.
7. You earn to spend.
8. The average American spends $1.20 for each dollar they earn. Don't make that mistake. Don't be average. Dare to be different.
9. A budget is simply a plan of what you expect your money to do for you. Some map out a night on the town with more care and detail than they do their retirement. When you don't have a plan, you're planning to fail.

NET WORTH FORM

CATEGORY	CURRENT VALUE
ASSETS	
Cash in Savings Accounts	
Cash in Checking Accounts	
Certificates of Deposit (CDs)	
Cash on Hand	
Money Market Accounts	
Money Owed to Me (Rent, Deposits, etc.)	
Cash Value of Life Insurance	
Savings Bonds (current value)	
Stocks	
Bonds	
Mutual Funds	
Vested Value of Stock Options	
Other Investments	
Individual Retirement Accounts (IRAs)	
Keogh Accounts	
401(k) or 403(b) Accounts	
Other Retirement Plans	
Market Value of Your Home	
TOTAL ASSETS	

NET WORTH FORM

CATEGORY	CURRENT VALUE
Market Value of Other Real Estate	
Blue Book Value of Cars/Trucks	
Boats, Planes, Other Vehicles	
Jewelry	
Collectibles	
Furnishings and Other Personal Property	
Other	
TOTAL ASSETS	

NET WORTH FORM

CATEGORY	CURRENT VALUE
LIABILITIES	
Mortgages	
Car Loans	
Bank Loans	
Student Loans	
Home Equity Loans	
Other Loans	
Credit Card Balances	
Real Estate Taxed Owed	
Income Taxes Owed	
Other Taxes Owed	
Other Debts	
TOTAL LIABILITIES	
NET WORTH (Total assets minus Total Liabilities)	

BUDGET WORKSHEET *HOW MUCH CAN YOU SAVE?*		
CATEGORY	PER MONTH	PER YEAR
YOUR INCOME		
Wages, Salary, and Commissions		
Dividends, Interest, and Capital Gains		
Annuities, Pensions, and Social Security (Self)		
Death Benefits from Estate		
Income on Real Property		
Other		
REAL INCOME		
YOUR EXPENSES		
Taxes		
Mortgage / Rent		
Food		
Medical Expenses		
Utilities		
Telephone		
Car		
Clothing		
Childcare		
Tuition / Education Expenses		

BUDGET WORKSHEET
HOW MUCH CAN YOU SAVE?

CATEGORY	PER MONTH	PER YEAR
Insurance Premiums		
Maintenance of Home		
Maintenance of Car		
Hobbies		
Entertainment		
Vacations		
Memberships / Professional Fees		
Gifts and Donations		
Loans / Credit Cards		
Other		
REAL EXPENSES		
Total Income		
(minus) Total Expenses		
TOTAL AVAILABLE FOR SAVINGS AND INVESTMENTS		

FINANCIAL PLANNING
NOTES

This Year's Goals

_____

_____

_____

_____

_____

_____

_____

Next Year's Goals

_____

_____

_____

_____

_____

_____

_____

_____

> **When you don't have a plan, you're planning to fail.**

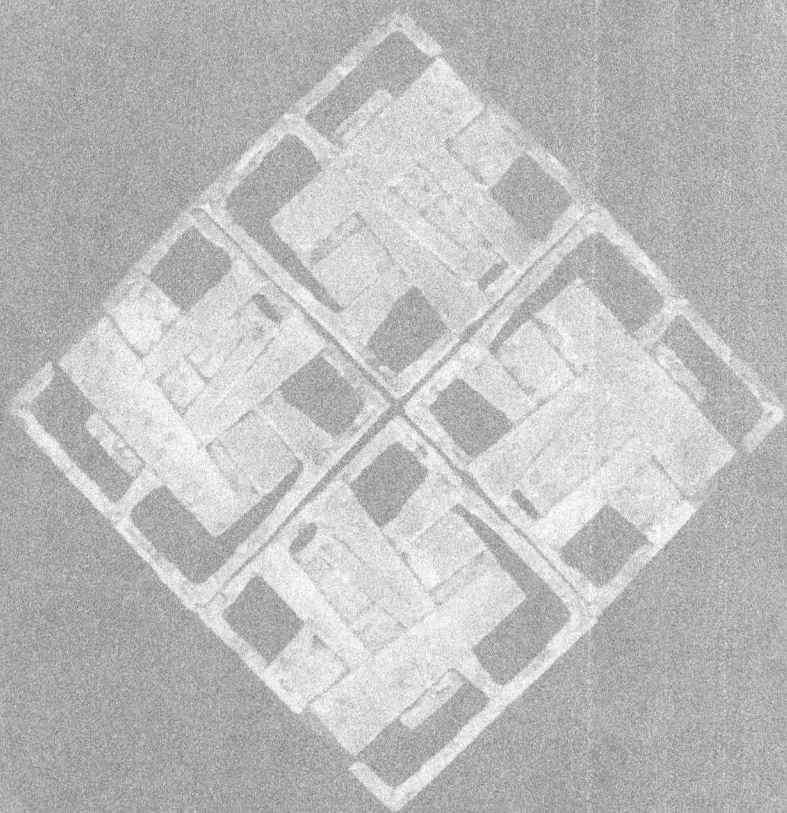

CHAPTER 2

Why Do I Need a Financial Advisor?

Trusted advisors are worth their weight in gold.
—Diva

"Diva, why do I need a Financial Advisor? I'm smart, successful, and own my own company. I'm a doctor, a lawyer, an engineer, a business owner, a politician, a professional athlete, etc. Why shouldn't I be able to do this on my own?"

The simple answer is that smart, successful people do what they do well—whether it is medicine, politics, or business—and they hire a good and competent financial advisor to help them create, implement, and monitor a financial strategy. As the 2020 DALBAR study[4] shows (S&P 500 graph on page 40), the S&P 500 Index beats the average equity fund investor by 1.81 percent. Most investors attempt to buy and sell based on what they see or hear is happening, which is often nothing more than an exercise in futility and frustration. They buy and sell at typically the precise *wrong* times. In other words, they buy and sell based on emotions instead of a fundamental investment philosophy. Diversification,

---

4 DALBAR, Inc. "Quantitative Analysis of Investor Behavior," For Period Ending December 31, 2019 (2020).

consistency, and discipline pay. One of the best things a good competent advisor will do for you is to help you minimize mistakes.

Research over the past two decades shows that investors too frequently buy and sell at sub-optimal times. The end result is that investors buy high, sell low, and earn significantly less than the market indices.

A CASE FOR A DISCIPLINED INVESTMENT PROCESS

Equity Market Returns vs. Equity Mutual Fund Investor Returns (2000-2019)

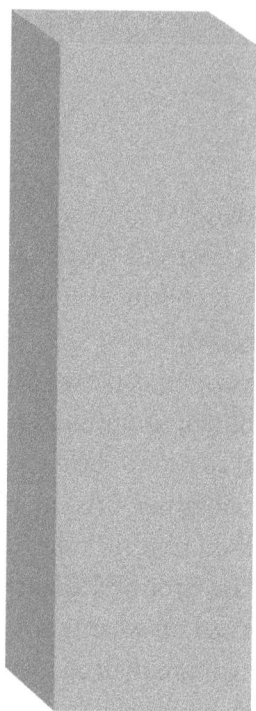

S&P 500 Index 6.06% annually	Avg. Equity Fund Investor 4.25% annually

DALBAR, Inc. "Quantitative Analysis of Investor Behavior," For Period Ending December 31, 2019. (2020).

THE CYCLE OF EMOTION

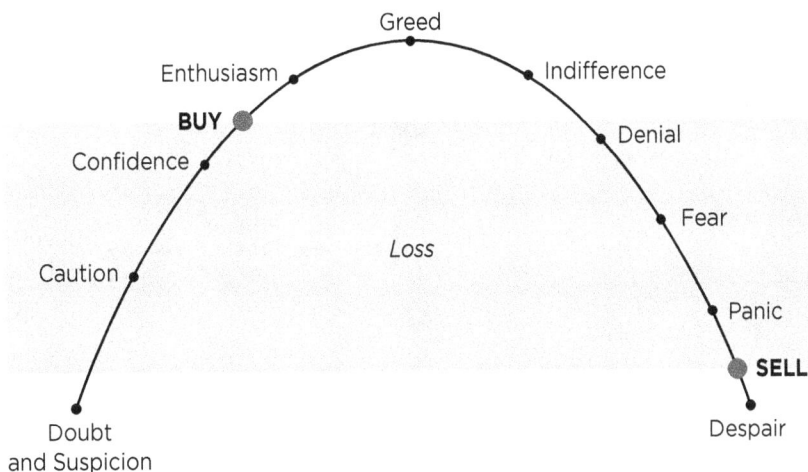

Greed

Enthusiasm — Indifference

BUY — Denial

Confidence

Fear

Loss

Caution

Panic

SELL

Doubt and Suspicion — Despair

Investing is your future—it's time for a new approach.
One in which discipline and expert advice are the
foundation of every investment decision.

Emotions and Your Money

One of the best illustrations I've ever seen of human nature is the "Cycle of Emotion"[5] when it comes to financial decisions.

We have all done it. Not to embarrass you, I will share *my* biggest "stupid" financial mistake. When I was twenty-seven, I had a beautiful Italian friend, Denise, whose husband, David, was in the securities business five years before I got into the financial industry. Denise told me about a "hot deal" David had. He was said to be making huge returns, turning $2,000 into $20,000 in no time at all. Skeptical at first, I thought about this with caution. Meanwhile, I watched while other people made the big score. I was certain I had seen enough. With a great deal of confidence and with great enthusiasm, I made the big decision to invest a meager life savings.

---

5 Investors Gone Bad: The Lessons of Behavioral Finance

PRIMARY TRUSTED ADVISOR CHART

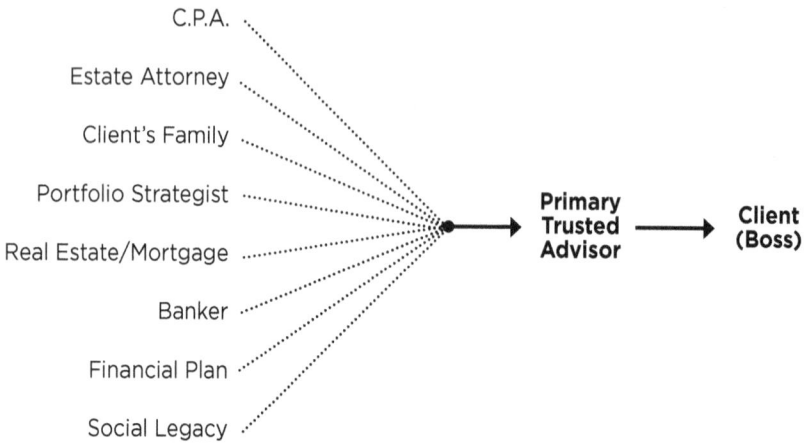

C.P.A.
Estate Attorney
Client's Family
Portfolio Strategist
Real Estate/Mortgage
Banker
Financial Plan
Social Legacy

→ **Primary Trusted Advisor** → **Client (Boss)**

Looking back now, I knew I had no reason to be confident, yet there I was jumping in with both feet.

You can guess what happened next. The deal promptly went south, and I lost it all. What happened? Quite simply, my greed overruled my brain.

"Education is expensive," and believe me I felt like I just earned an advanced degree. Luckily, I didn't blame my friend's husband or the investment. I could only point the finger at one person: myself and my greed for a get-rich-quick deal.

There are two life lessons to be learned here. First, only invest in those things that have been explained clearly and make common sense to you. Make sure the investments are in line with your risk tolerance and investment goals. Second, consistency will always outperform occasional brilliance. I decided then and there to never, I mean never, invest in a "hot deal" when I know virtually nothing about it.

And I haven't invested in a "hot deal" since. I've been telling my clients the same thing for over twenty-five years now. Do not invest in something you do not understand or that doesn't make sense to you. Seek advice from a team of investment managers who possess impressive credentials, substantial research capabilities, and longstanding records of success. *This advice alone* may be enough to save you many hundreds of thousands of dollars!

Investing should not be like a trip to the car dealership. Nobody is going to get the manager to see how they can "get you into that car today, little lady."

If an investment plan is good today, it should be good tomorrow. Do not misunderstand. It's not possible for you to know everything there is to know about "the industry." Your advisor should be experienced and competent enough to clearly explain the benefits, the suitability of the investment choices available to you, and how those choices will help you achieve your goals and objectives once they are clarified.

I am not referring to a slick "sales pitch." I am referring to a paid professional assisting you in making wise decisions and preventing you from making bad decisions. There is a big difference.

You can learn a lot by knowing the difference between a trusted financial advisor and someone interested in only selling the financial product of the day.

Emotions Are Not an Investment Strategy

A great, hard-working friend of many years came to me for advice. He had amassed $50 million in real estate holdings. He wanted my recommendation on a restaurant investment and sent over information. Fortunately, I knew the people to call. I sat down with my friend and explained "the real reason" he wanted to participate in this venture. It was emotional. He was interested in the celebrity types who were listed as investors, and they made him feel very special to be considered in another group of ten outside investors. I offered him the following recommendation: "If you do not care about your investment and just want to have 'bragging rights' to be in this group, then maybe that's a good enough reason.

Otherwise, based on the research I've shared with you, at this particular time, this may be a good investment for someone else, but not for you."

Mid-tier Millionaires Want Just One Trusted Primary Advisor

Even when you're successful and have a portfolio worth millions, you still need a trusted financial advisor. In the industry, we call this the "mid-tier millionaire" paradox or the MTMs—people who try to manage their wealth worth between $5 million and $30 million. Investors with more money generally can afford to run what the industry calls "a family or private office," to delegate money decisions on a full-time basis.

Those who are between $1 million and $5 million, although affluent in most parts of the country, don't have the kind of wealth to trigger complex financial decisions. Yet MTMs are facing many decisions. They crave finding that one person they can go to and get solid advice and who can assemble the team they need to manage their wealth.

The primary advisor that's suitable for you can deal with investment management, accountants, lawyers, banks, wire houses, family members, clients, and others who can have a direct impact on the mid-tier millionaire. Picture a symphony conductor in an orchestra pit, and you might have an idea of the kind of person I'm talking about. This primary advisor orchestrates the coordination of all the individual parts (musicians) to produce complete harmony, thereby providing you, the client, an organized accounting of the management and progress of your assets/wealth. In many cases, the MTM simply doesn't have the time or expertise to deal with the plethora of entities involved in their portfolio.

Top Three Things MTMs Want

Unlike millionaires with $1-5 million, whose primary goal is to partner with a trusted *investment* advisor, the MTM must also find a trusted *primary* advisor—who more often than not is also the trusted

Investment Advisor—with broad knowledge as well as investment knowledge. This advisor acts as a symphony conductor, coordinating a team of advisors who have professional processes and offer support. MTMs seek the following three things when looking for an advisor:

- **Transparency.** They want to know what services each advisor is providing. They might ask, "What am I paying for each service, and is it fair compensation?" MTMs aren't looking for the least expensive; they're looking for the "best."
- **Collaboration.** A primary advisor can collaborate with bankers, accountants, lawyers, etc., who are not necessarily all in the same location. This is done with secure online access to client information.
- **Aggregation or simplicity in reporting.** MTMs don't have the time to accumulate and decipher reports from various providers, bankers, investment advisors, CPAs, and attorneys. These reports must be easily readable and show an evaluation of the MTM's financial progress in an easy-to-understand fashion.

The Baby Boomer Challenge

Baby boomers are the 78 million people the U.S. Census tells us were born between 1946 and 1964. It's likely that you're a member of this group yourself.

The entire retirement scene has changed for baby boomers. At one time, retirement was strictly by the numbers. A valued employee would turn sixty-five, get a gold watch, and head off to his white-picket-fence home to sit in his rocking chair on his front porch to live out his days on earth. He would have earned some kind of modest pension with his company. Together, with social security and a paid off home, he and his wife would live happily ever after. Growing up, most baby boomers probably thought this was their fate as well.

Although some may believe this will still happen, this fairy tale retirement isn't part of the baby boomers' future. We all must face the raw truth concerning life in the new millennium. Couple the dollar numbers with longer life expectancies—it won't be unusual for the post-World-War II generation to live thirty years or more after retirement. How many have actually planned for this reality?

According to Benjamin Stein of the National Retirement Planning Coalition[6], "Tens of millions of Americans are seriously under-prepared to meet their financial needs in retirement." As many as forty percent of Americans have saved almost nothing for retirement.

Allstate Financial Services did a survey recently and found 37 percent of baby boomers will be financially responsible for either parents or children during retirement. Seven percent will be paying for both parents and children. Furthermore, during retirement, many will be paying off credit card debt, mortgages, and car notes.

The No. 1 Retirement Rule

Here's the Diva's No. 1 rule for baby boomers and all retirees. Do not go into retirement with bad debt.

Want to avoid this? Do yourself a favor. Find a trusted advisor. Between the two of you, draw a road map that leads from wherever you are to retirement. Make sure that road isn't lined with bad debt. Make sure you also create a substantial nest egg, which can carry you through what could possibly be decades of retirement, whether you want to spend your retirement years surfing, rock climbing, golfing, or traveling the world. How you plan today determines how you live once retired. Retirement should be your golden years. Without the gold, these years could be a challenge to your peace of mind and your happiness.

---

6 Benjamin Stein. Statement of Ben Stein, Honorary Chairperson. The National Retirement Planning Coalition. February 25, 2004.

THE DIVA'S ADVICE

1. When it comes to taking the right financial steps in life, get together with someone who has the expertise to help you make the right decisions. Yes, it is time-consuming. What's the alternative? Becoming a greeter at some department store?

2. Everyone has a bad money story, which still stings years later. I had my turn chasing after the "hot deal." If you don't have all the facts or if the deal doesn't make sense, don't leap. An advisor is there to help you understand the risks and rewards.

3. Mid-tier millionaires may seem like they have it made with wealth estimated between $5 million and $30 million. Nothing could be further from the truth! They crave having a primary advisor who can work together with all the institutions, CPAs, tax attorneys, trust attorneys, and other parties to make sense of their portfolio. A trusted advisor is a necessity for this class. The truth is that everyone can benefit financially from sound, solid fiscal advice.

4. Run—don't walk—to a financial advisor if you're a baby boomer. This group isn't good at saving, and they're facing a retirement that may last for more than thirty years. Make plans now.

5. Do not even consider being in debt while retired.

6. Have I scared you into action? Good! I would rather encourage and inspire. And if it takes fear to wake you up, then I hope this book will be your wake-up call.

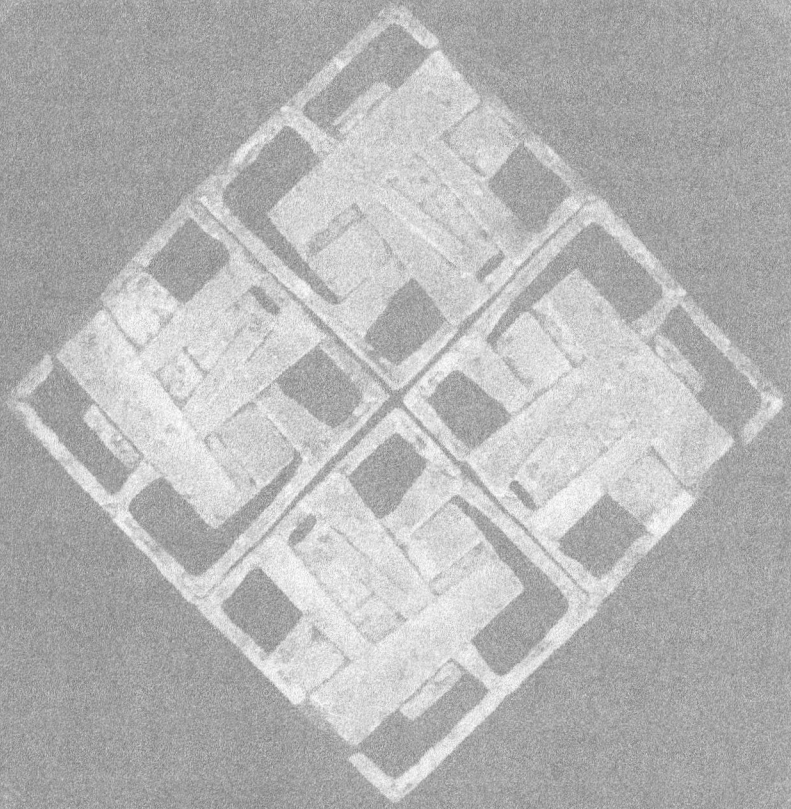

CHAPTER 3

Who Is a Financial Advisor?

Talk is cheap. It takes $Money to buy champagne.
—Diva

Everyone seems to think they are your financial advisor these days. Your banker, your life insurance agent, your health insurance agent, your CPA, your property and casualty agent, your stockbroker, and even your trust attorney may all think they are your financial advisors. I even heard a real estate professional claim she was someone's financial advisor. It's mind boggling! In reality, most of these individuals are simply salespeople with a product to sell.

"My banker is a salesperson? I don't think so, Victoria!" Oh, really? You think not? Let me share a story—just one of many I could use to illustrate this point.

One day, I was sitting in my temporary office on the property where I constructed our new 5,000-square-foot building in the Financial District of Oklahoma. It was a gorgeous sunny day, and my receptionist announced to me we had two visitors—the CEO and the vice president from a major, very successful bank. They didn't have an appointment and they just dropped by unexpectedly.

This was a bit surprising. I had to chuckle to myself since these were two very important and busy gentlemen just "dropping by to visit."

I had the pleasure of doing business with these gentlemen on several occasions previously, and they epitomize professionalism. I cannot stress enough how much respect I have for them and how important these businessmen have been, and are, to the growth of my company and our community. For them to spontaneously drop by for a visit was more than a bit surprising. So I stopped what I was doing and invited them into my office.

I had them sit down and then called all the office girls to the door of my office. I announced to them, "These are two VERY important gentlemen. Their time is too valuable to just drop by to visit. What they're really here for is to sell us some money!" The look on these men's faces was, in a word, "priceless"! We all got a chuckle out of it, and the girls went back to work.

Typically, most people dread going to their bankers when they need a loan, whether it be to start up or expand a business. Why? Because most people find the process of asking for money humiliating and, as a result, see themselves as being a step or two above being a beggar. In addition, the applicants must provide the bank with reams of personal information in order to convince them to approve the loan. Their future rests in the hands of the bank, which can grant or deny the loan as they see fit—just like Caesar: "Thumbs up or thumbs down, off with their heads." So it's a great position to be in when bankers come to you asking to loan you money. That was the scenario I faced that day with my important visitors.

I opened the conversation with, "So you're selling money today? Exactly how much do you want to sell me?" The answer was, "How much do you want, Victoria?" The fact was, I had a great deal of equity in this particular piece of land and my buildings. These properties were almost 100 percent debt free and clearly mine. The CEO responded, "Well, how much would you like? $800,000? $1 million? $1.2 million?"

"Well," I said, "I might be in the market. Just exactly how much are you selling money for today?"

So Who Truly Is a Trusted Financial Advisor?

What qualifies me to answer this question? Allow me to share my credentials. I am an independent insurance agent—life, accident, and health—specializing in life insurance, long-term care, and fixed annuities. I held a securities license as a registered representative for more than ten years, and I am also an Investment Advisor Representative. Based on my experience, education, and training, I am well qualified to explain to you the differences in how each of these entities function.

An investment advisor is a fiduciary—advisors acting in the best interest of their clients and disclosing any real or implied conflicts of interest. There is generally a higher standard for a fiduciary than is customary in the financial services industry. In contrast, an insurance agent's main responsibility is to the insurance company.

My relationship has been and is always with my clients and what's in their best interest. When I have had to call an insurance company, I fought on behalf of my client. When I was taking my insurance test, one of the questions was, "Who is your loyalty to?" For test purposes, and test purposes only, the answer was "to the insurance company." I remember this question because I strongly disagreed with it.

Not all states have as high of standards and extensive training and licensing requirements as does Oklahoma. That's not a good thing. Those of us in the industry actually joke that in some states, you can be a "dog catcher" one day and an "insurance professional" the next day.

Typically, an insurance agent who sells fixed annuity products earns a one time commission. That is a one time sale, and the agent then moves on to the next sale—this is called a transaction business model. That is similar to the professional activities of most sales professions. It's all sales and no service. That's not for me. I work for and with my clients who are my first priority.

The story of a dear client comes to mind. She was one of my first accounts. She had a 401(k) account with substantial funds and wanted some of her money guaranteed, no matter what. This is what I call *sacred money.* Sometimes it has been inherited from a parent, and a client wants it guaranteed. My client selected a product that offered an immediate bonus with market rate interest. Several years later after she purchased it, she called the office and told my assistant that she wanted to surrender her policy because she did not like the fact that she could not take her accumulated value at any time in a lump sum. Her current surrender value was substantially less. I returned her call, and she informed me the insurance company told her she could never take out a lump sum. I explained to her that she might have misunderstood because under certain circumstances, I felt sure she could take her lump sum. This is what I refer to as "Greeks talking to Romans." She is a Roman, and the insurance company is Greek. I, on the other hand, speak both languages. I told her I wanted to call the insurance company on her behalf and verify her options.

I confirmed with the insurance company that if she could take interest only for a period of time and then her lump sum, she would come out much better than surrendering it all at once. Furthermore, I requested this in writing. Nothing verbal will do for the Diva in situations like this. The insurance company immediately provided the information in writing. My client then chose not to surrender her policy and thanked me repeatedly for taking the time to clarify this for her and getting it in writing. This is the big difference a trusted financial advisor can make. I congratulated her for being smart enough to call me before making a mistake and also for giving me the opportunity to assist her. In short, some solid advice from a qualified financial advisor saved her from making a costly financial mistake.

Clients must use caution in these situations because the insurance agent is unlikely to do it for them. Since the insurance agents have received their commissions on the initial sale, it's not unusual for them to just send you a copy of the requested surrender form. This process usually takes less than three minutes to do, and then the agent's obligations are fulfilled. Is it really in the best interest of the client? Absolutely not. Therefore, investors should not be surprised when agents do not act in an investment advisor capacity, which works on a fee-base, much like a retainer.

A registered representative is often referred to as a broker. Brokers/registered representatives are regulated by the National Association of Securities Dealers (NASD) and must adhere to the rule known as suitability. That simply requires a broker to know minimal information about their client and gain financial information before making specific investment recommendations. Brokers are typically known for selling stocks, bonds, and mutual funds. Generally, brokers spend a lot of time on the telephone contacting prospects about a stock, bond, or mutual fund. When they're not on the phone with prospective clients, they're not earning any commission or money. Financial professionals call this "smilin' and dialin'."

A constant complaint I get from investors during their initial consultation is that they cannot get a return telephone call from their "financial advisor"—this is the client's term. The more proper title is broker or insurance agent. The brutally honest explanation for why brokers are not returning the call is because there isn't any money for simply servicing an account. They only earn money when they are selling stocks, bonds, and mutual funds and executing a trade. (Executing a trade is a fancy term for taking an order.) Servicing clients is low on a broker's list of priorities. This business model is not customer friendly. The problem comes from a client's expectation of consultative services that are not part of the model.

Not everyone wants to have the kind of relationship with their clients that an independent Investment Advisor Representative does. That is why it is important to find the appropriate advisor for your goals, objectives, and circumstances.

In my more than twenty-five years of experience, I have discovered that the only type of advisor I would use as an investor is an Investment Advisor Representative from an Independent Registered Investment Advisor firm. (ChappelWood Financial Services is an Independent Registered Investment Advisor firm registered in the state of Oklahoma.)

With this business model, the investor pays the "fee-based" advisor a percentage of their portfolio assets each year, which is as low as .50 to 2.5 percent, depending on the services provided by the advisory firm, and the assets invested. They may also earn compensation on a flat rate or hourly fee. The investment advisor is also a fiduciary or advisor acting in the best interest of their clients and disclosing any real or implied conflicts of interest. You can see why it is in your best interest to have a fiduciary rather than a salesperson as your true "financial advisor."

As an independent insurance agent, I never have been obligated to any company to meet quotas or sales goals. When determining needs for clients, I shop the market for the best product to meet their needs. Independent insurance companies are always introducing new fixed annuity products. It's frustrating that the insurance companies never provide a client profile for the product being introduced.

I, however, want to know the profile of the type of client this product was designed for to determine if it is truly appropriate for my clients. I need to know if I want to market that product to specific clients. For example, one product may be appropriate for doctors, while another would be more suitable for teachers or manufacturers. Their needs vary and one size does not fit all. The reason companies do not provide a client profile is because it's not to their benefit. Remember, It's *All* About The $Money, Honey!® The companies want all agents to make the product fit the agent's niche market, whatever that market might be.

The Issue of Incentives

You need to be aware that companies often dangle carrots before their sales forces. Companies provide incentives for stockbrokers and insurance agents, such as bonuses, vacations, or other benefits, for selling specific mutual funds and/or annuity products. These incentives are not required to be disclosed to the investor. You can see how this could be a possible conflict. How would you know whether the product is appropriate for you or when it's just a good sale for the sales agent?

For example, early in my financial services career, I began as an independent insurance agent. A regional representative (we'll call him "Ron") from a major insurance company came to shadow, or watch, me for a day. After his visit, I was invited to the corporate office to have lunch with him and his boss, who was the president of sales, who, during a lovely lunch, congratulated me and told me how pleased he was that I would be joining them on their cruise.

Surprised, I said, "Cruise?" Ron gave me a gentle nudge under the table, indicating to me to just follow along. "You know, the Billion Dollar Bash Cruise," the president said. I responded, "Oh, yes," and then changed the subject. I obviously did not have a clue about this cruise, and I was supporting Ron by pretending I did. We then went for a tour of their office, and Ron explained to me about this year-long contest. Although I had been unaware of it, I qualified for the cruise based on the number of applications I had submitted.

Can you see how these types of conflicts of interest could jeopardize recommendations you're given? It's obvious I was not influenced by the incentive since I was clueless of its existence. I was simply doing my job.

However, there are agents who are tempted by these incentives and, unfortunately, put them ahead of their clients' needs. It should be noted that nothing is wrong with incentives as long as the needs of the client are the reason for the recommendations and not the incentive alone. It should be known that if an Investment Advisor Representative were to be offered any kind of incentive, they are legally bound to disclose this due to a possible conflict of interest. As stated earlier, however, stockbrokers and insurance agents are not required or obligated to disclose the information to the investor.

In summary, an Investment Advisor Representative is an advisor acting in a consulting capacity rather than a transactional capacity. If you are still a little confused about this terminology, you are not alone. Sometimes I think the industry makes it intentionally confusing. Just remember that an Independent Investment Advisor Representative functions in a fiduciary capacity, is generally held to a higher standard, and is legally obligated to disclose any real or potential conflict of interest. It's my opinion that this person should be clearly acting in your interest. That's the way it should be (see graph).

TYPICAL BUSINESS MODELS

Transactional	Opinion	Relationship
Shopper	Customer	Client
One Time Sale	Annual Sale	Consistent Monitoring
Transaction Oriented	Fee Oriented	Relationship Oriented
No Service	Annual Service	Full Service
One Time	Annual	Lifetime
Handles 1000s	Manages 500s-1000s	Provides unique experience for 100-150
Cautious	Trusted	Most Trusted

Set reasonable expectations from your providers.

THE DIVA'S ADVICE

1. Many professionals claim to be "financial advisors." Most aren't. Some basic understanding of the roles and objectives of those in the financial industry can be beneficial to you. How beneficial? It may mean several hundreds of thousands of dollars, or millions, plus some sound investing decisions.

2. Bankers have sound financial advice. They play a vital role in commerce.

3. Insurance agents sell a product. After the initial sale, it may no longer be in their interest to service the customer. A true financial advisor, such as an Independent Investment Advisor Representative should look at what's best for the client. Beware. Without the advice of a professional, it could cost you money.

4. The term "fiduciary" is important to know. A fiduciary is required to disclose any possible conflicts of financial interest.

5. Brokers are most interested in the sale. They are involved in "smilin' and dialin'" on the telephone and may be driven more by quotas than doing what's right for their clients.

6. Some in the financial industry are not only motivated by sales but also given extra incentives. An insurance agent or stockbroker isn't required to let you know about these extras. A fiduciary is required to.

7. If you're looking for a long-term relationship with a true financial advisor, go with an Independent Registered Investment Advisor. They're held to a higher standard, which is good news for you.

8. Remember that a primary advisor is much like a primary care physician. Other members of the health community help to nurse you back to health; the primary physician, however, is the one who takes charge. The same is true with your finances. The bankers, brokers, and others have a role to play; it's the primary advisor who charts the course for your portfolio.

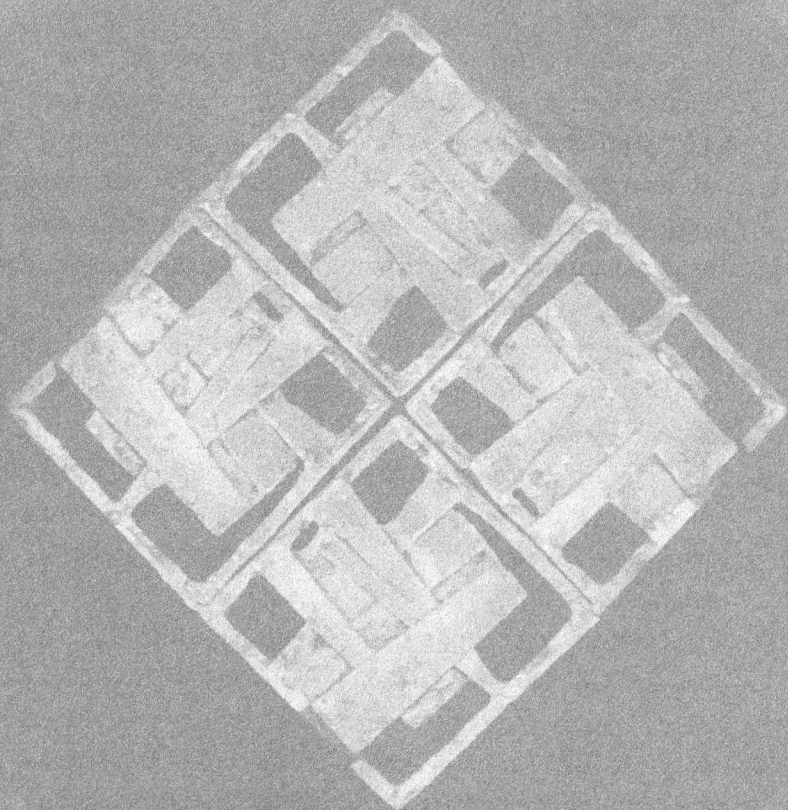

CHAPTER 4

How Do I Find a Financial Advisor?

"Fast is great; accuracy is everything."
— Wyatt Earp

Since you've made the wise investment to read this book, you're climbing one or more steps of your own personal money ladder. Maybe your oil company was just bought out or you're wanting to rollover your 401(k). Or perhaps you're preparing for an inheritance you're about to receive. You might have money to invest, or you're retired. Maybe you need advice to reach a safe, prosperous retirement. Whatever step you're on now, you're spending your time reading this to help educate yourself on the best way to be a good steward of your money. You feel it is your obligation and responsibility to yourself, your family, and your community. Congratulations!

First the Bad News: It's a Minefield Out There!

The financial industry is not just complicated; it is extremely complicated! It's complex, confusing, and has many, many layers. (Visualize the layers of the Earth, and you just might have a vague idea.) It can take a lifetime in this industry to get a handle on the "do's and don'ts" of money and investing. Certainly, the media does not help. I recently had a radio show listener call and ask me, "Diva, how do you know what to believe? I watch all the money shows on Saturday morning, and I am more confused than ever."

First of all, it's television! By its nature, television is entertainment. That's why nobody seems to agree on anything. Who would tune in? Sadly, this media outlet must be confrontational to draw and keep an audience. It's no wonder highly intelligent, successful people hesitate to venture into this minefield! Bureaucracy and unscrupulous people have helped to make the financial arena even more complicated. In 1997, it only took three pages to open an account, whether you opened it with $2,000 or $20 million. Now it's twenty-eight pages or more!

Personally, I cannot imagine going through this minefield alone. When you're making financial decisions, the best thing you can do is rely on a professional financial advisor's experience and knowledge. Basic questions and principles will arm you with the right knowledge, so you will have confidence in the decisions you and your financial advisor make.

Finding the Perfect Financial Advisor

Finding the right financial advisor can be a challenge. In my opinion, it can be as hard as moving to a new city and finding a new hairdresser, physician, or trusted mechanic. There is no way to make this easy for you. This is one thing you must invest some time in because this should be a long-term relationship. The quality of your life, children's education, your retirement, and the protection of your assets depend on it. Less than 39 percent of investors use the services of advisors. That certainly explains why the average investor receives substantially less return than the S&P 500 Index.

These statistics alone should be enough to ignite you to want to make selecting your advisor your No. 1 priority! Believe it or not, you can recover from one botched hair appointment or a poor automobile repair. The wrong financial advisor, however, may cost you your family fortune or your children's education. If you're lucky, it could mean you *only* lose tens of thousands of dollars. In a worst-case scenario, you might be saying goodbye to your retirement plans or leaving your heirs a much-depleted inheritance and no legacy at all. *Selecting the right advisor is vital.*

The reason most people are afraid to find a financial advisor is because they don't even know the right questions to ask. Fortunately, there is good news. Those days of not knowing what questions to ask or what to look for are over.

Following are some criteria to use to give you confidence that you're asking the right questions.

Questions the Financial Diva Would Ask When Hiring a Financial Advisor

1. May I have a copy of your Uniform Application for Investment Adviser Registration (ADV)? You only want an advisor that is an independent Investment Advisor Representative with an independent Registered Investment Advisory firm. Please note the word "independent." That's much different from a wire house. The way to quickly get to this point is to ask them for a copy of their ADV—this document fully explains who the company is and the background of the advisors as well as services they provide and fees. I would specifically want to know if financial planning services are available for a separate fee. This is an objective plan that you purchase and can take to any advisor and implement any or all of the recommendations. If you get any hesitation about their ADV, or if they do not provide objective financial plans separately for a fee, then beware! Please move on to the next advisor.

2. What are your qualifications? Independent Investment Advisors' qualifications are important. Find out if they also have been licensed in insurance, securities, mortgage field, or real estate. Ask how long they have actively held licenses in those fields. In my opinion, five years minimum is a good starting point. The

education required for these licenses and ongoing continuing education is extensive. I doubt you want your nest egg being managed by someone just getting started with you as the guinea pig, so find out how much experience they have as an independent Investment Advisor Representative—just how long have they been in the financial industry? Do they have roots? Do they own their own building, or do they lease space? Or can they pick up and leave for Guatemala at a moment's notice without any notification? Are they involved in their community? Think of the things that are important to you as an individual as well, such as: do they participate in charities, the Church, or the Chamber of Commerce?

3. What is your process? What is the advisor's investment philosophy? What you want to ask is, "Are you a one-man shop who thinks he is the next Peter Lynch?" Are you going to entrust all your money with someone who thinks he can outperform the top portfolio strategist in the world? The advisor's answer should be: "We analyze our clients' needs, goals, and objectives and create strategies and solutions to meet your goals, objectives, and tolerance to risk. We offer the top portfolio strategists who have a disciplined approach and have a long history of success available in an open architecture platform." You want the best strategist available for the amount of money you have to invest, because your goal is to give yourself the best chance for long-term success. If an advisor wants to "sell" you something at your first meeting, you are probably going to want to move on down the road.

4. What market is your specialty? Whether you are a doctor, small business owner, or farmer, you want to work with an advisor who already understands your industry's market, business, and special needs. Ask if the advisor has a breakdown of his or her client profiles. In our case at ChappelWood Financial, we have an Ideal Client Profile, so our clients know who and what we specialize in.

5. How are you compensated? Advisors are paid in various ways. Payment can range from hourly to a fee-based percentage of assets managed, to a commission, a retainer, or a flat project rate. The advisor's ADV should spell this out for you as well. The answer to your question should be, "I can be compensated by all these methods. It is based on the needs and suitability of each client and the solutions to their unique situation. You will know the recommended solution, the options, and the cost to you before we ever proceed with any implementation."

6. Do you have a team approach? Most seasoned financial professionals have a team of people they call on as needed for their clients. When the need is small, this can be a professional courtesy where there is no cost involved; however, when extensive services are required, you should pay for their advice as needed. It is comforting to know you have their experience to draw on. Don't be fooled just because someone you interview has many advisors in one office, as they may just be leasing office space. Bigger is not always better. You may receive much more personal service in a smaller firm. The majority of our business comes from dissatisfied wire house clients. I couldn't tell you one client that has come to me from an independent Investment Advisor Representative. That is clear confirmation to me that this method is meeting the needs of investors today. Also, be aware that many wire houses have begun Registered Investment Advisor (RIA) arms that would not be considered independent.

7. Have you ever filed for personal or business bankruptcy? Legally, as an independent Registered Investment Advisor Representative (RIA), this is required to be disclosed. Who would know if it's not disclosed? You should ask the question. If they have filed bankruptcy, do you really want them managing your money when they cannot manage their own? Is there any reasonable explanation? It's your money; you be the judge. Don't take advice from broke people.

8. What can you tell me about your Errors and Omissions (E&O) policy? A trusted financial advisor should carry this insurance policy in the event of an inadvertent error or possible omission, which can cost a client. Make sure your advisor has this coverage. This insurance is as important to a financial advisor as homeowner or car insurance is to the average person. Not having this E&O policy is just irresponsible.

9. How many clients do you have? The answer should be no more than 150. If they brag about 500 or 1000, beware! How could they possibly monitor your account and provide you premier service?

10. Do you have a guarantee? It might read similar to ChappelWood Financial Services' guarantee (see page 65).

A Kudos for Women

If you are a woman, I must give you a special congratulations and a pat on the back. First, research shows you are more likely to seek professional advice than men. Does that make us smarter? Only the most successful and smartest of men are confident enough with themselves to hire competent female advisors.

Studies show that you believe you require $5 million to $10 million to live comfortably in retirement and are using advisors in order to achieve your goals. You are different from men—I bet that's not the first time you've heard that! You're not as concerned about your advisors' gender, school affiliation, sports preferences, or cars they drive. The bottom line for you is that you want your advisors to listen and, more importantly, hear you. You want them to have the knowledge, compassion, and skills to guide you in making the right decisions to achieve your goals.

What you have in common with your male counterpart is that you want to trust your advisor. I applaud you! I, however, am so lucky to have the best male clients ever. They are smart, successful, confident businessmen, lawyers, NFL referees, and doctors.

I am selective when it comes to new clients. I decided on one criterion that is the most important: "People I enjoy working with!" Because of my requirements, I have the most interesting, knowledgeable, and best clients—male and female—and I thank all my clients for allowing me the pleasure of being their trusted primary advisor.

THE DIVA'S ADVICE

1. Finding a financial advisor is like a minefield. The best way to get through it is to be armed with the proper questions.
2. Know the right questions to ask a potential advisor. Don't be shy about asking for qualifications. It's your money, and the wrong advisor may cost you dearly.
3. Ask about their investment philosophy.
4. What market is their specialty? Doctors have different needs from retirees.
5. Has the advisor filed bankruptcy? If so, this is a huge red flag for someone wanting to handle your money.
6. A special kudos to women. They generally seek advice concerning money management more than men.

CHAPPELWOOD FINANCIAL SERVICES

We guarantee that as a client of CFS you will consistently receive Premium Service delivered in a timely manner. We promise to organize the financial part of your life and develop specific communications that meet your personality and needs. While we cannot guarantee investment performance, we do guarantee your satisfaction with our service. If CFS does not perform to your satisfaction, inform me immediately. I will resolve any issue to your approval. We are irreplaceable to our clients.

Victoria L. Woods, Chief Investment Advisor
President/CEO

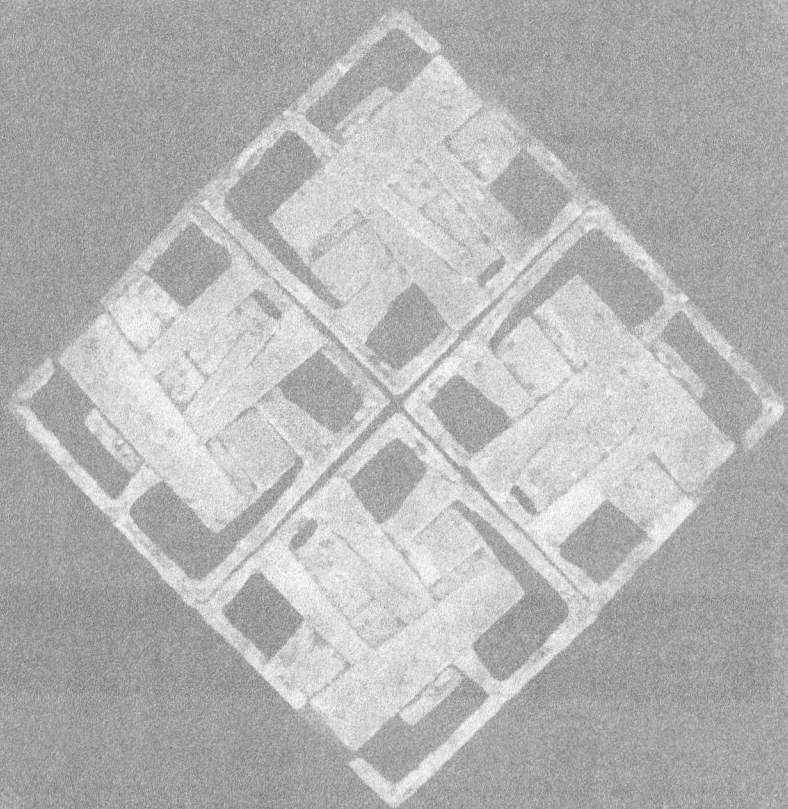

CHAPTER 5

What Should I Expect from a Financial Advisor?

"Where there is no vision, the people perish."
– Proverbs 29:18

Learning from ChappelWood's Model

Every time someone in our industry visits my office, the first question I usually get is, "From which wire house did you get your start?" It's always "shock and awe" at my answer when I tell them I've never worked for a wire house or one of the bigger financial firms.

My career started as an independent insurance agent, specializing in annuity and life insurance. I then became an independent registered representative, specializing in mutual funds. As my experience and knowledge increased, I became an independent Investment Advisor Representative, specializing as a fee-based investment/financial advisor in a consultant capacity for high net-worth investors. You could say I value my independence. Was it easy to start this way? No way! Luckily for me, I didn't know any better. Everyone I know in the industry wishes they could go back and start over knowing what they know now. They unanimously believe they could better serve their clients if they were independent and didn't have to deal with the politics and the constraints of the bigger companies.

After more than twenty years in the financial industry, I have asked a lot of questions and discovered common complaints from my clients concerning dealing with a major wire house—complaints such as:

- "I cannot reach my advisor."
- "They only call when they want to sell me something."
- "I don't understand my statements."
- "I don't know if I have made money or not."
- "I don't know if my performance is on par with the market."
- "My advisor talks over my head using terminology I do not understand, making me feel ignorant and inferior."
- "I don't feel comfortable asking the advisor questions."

I have spent my career designing my company, ChappelWood Financial Services, around solving these problems for investors. I was taught early on, "Find a need and fill it." It seems very simple. It's not always easy, yet it's simple. My hope is that my findings will give you the insights needed to make the right decision when hiring a financial advisor. Remember, it's a big decision and I wish you success.

ChappelWood's Values and Processes

Contacting Your Advisor

At ChappelWood Financial Services, we have an actual person or a direct voice mail to answer each call. We prefer this rather than the frustrating recordings that send you to seven different extensions before failing to connect you to the person you need. Our goal is to answer the call by the fourth ring. If everyone is on a call with a client, we pledge to return the call within twenty-four hours of every workday. My staff is very well-trained and qualified to answer most questions before they ever get to me.

Your Statements

When investors say they are unable to understand their statements, believe me, I can relate. Some of the statements take me hours to decipher! I feel your pain. I have made it my business to provide reports that are easy to understand. It took me years to accomplish this goal. Your performance statements/quarterly reports should be as easy to understand as your checkbook or a grade school report card. As a third grader, you knew exactly where you stood if you got a "B" on a math test. Statements reflecting your investments and your money should be as easy to read and understand.

ChappelWood clients are pleased that they can actually understand their performance account statements. When they relocate out of state, I encourage them to look for a local advisor—someone they can sit down with face to face. To my surprise, they refuse. Our processes are so easy that they can check on their accounts and quarterly statements online from anywhere in the world. You would think this would be the industry standard—it's not.

SAMPLE STATEMENT—EASY TO READ

As of March 31, 2021

Portfolio Summary

	Beginning Market Value	Net Contributions & Withdrawals	Portfolio Gain/ Loss	Ending Market Value
CURRENT QUARTER	$1,725,752.42	$90,000.00	$27,378.46	$1,843,130.88
ANNUALLY				
2020	$500,000.00	$1,056.293.27	$170,459.15	$1,725,752.42
2021	$1,725,752.42	$90,000.00	$27,378.46	$1,843,130.88
SINCE INCEPTION	$500,000.00	$1,145,293.27	$197,837.61	$1,843,130.88

Communication

As stated before, "The Financial Diva" also figuratively speaks the financial languages of Greek, Roman, and English. Therefore, I can effectively communicate with our clients in a language they understand—English.

I have made it my top priority to speak in plain English. I always encourage my clients to stop the discussion when they are unclear about anything. (You have my permission to do the same with your advisor.) As an advisor, it's up to me to clarify the options. If I ever begin speaking in an unknown language such as Greek, there is nothing wrong with stopping me for a translation. That applies to discussions in my office, during a speaking engagement, or on my weekly radio show. This process is a two-way communication. When you don't understand, nobody wins.

Consistency Over Occasional Brilliance

I believe strongly in constant improvement. I am constantly complimented on ChappelWood's service. At the same time, I know there is always room for improvement. I believe so strongly in this that each Friday we close the office to the public early and meet for ongoing training and discussions to improve service and processes for our clients.

Initial Process for Our Ideal Clients

My experience has shown that this process is best for our clients, their families, and my staff. What we know is that clients are doing something with their money every day.

What we do, and what your advisor should do, is develop an action plan and strategy for your financial organization and management. After that, we make sure everybody—from the spouse to the CPA and attorney—is clear on what the plan is, who's responsible, and when the action will be taken. (See Action Plans on pages 72 and 73.)

Obviously, I can't share all the proprietary information about our unique company, so what I am divulging will give you a good idea of what you should expect.

Client Process

When prospective clients call my office, they either have been referred to me by one of our delighted clients or raving fans who heard about me from television, radio, or the print media. In other words, they know a great deal about me and my reputation before calling. You might not have that same opportunity when searching for your advisor.

The following is my client process. You should expect the same from the advisor you hire.

ChappelWood Process

During the initial consultation, my assistant takes basic information and requests statements and a self-discovery questionnaire to be completed. (You want the advisor to request this.) This saves everyone a lot of time. The advisor then needs to invest time in reviewing your goals and objectives. From this review, both of us can be realistic in setting expectations and evaluating whether or not this could be a good partnership. With so much at stake in your financial future, I believe it could be one of the most important partnerships you have.

Discovery/Financial Analysis

When I meet with a couple or an individual, I expect to have a very long-term relationship by obtaining a clear picture of their financial position, goals, objectives, and tolerance for risk. This is the first step in determining if it's going to be a beneficial partnership. *A customer is a one time sale. A client is an ongoing relationship.* If the client is sixty-five years old, I fully expect to be their advisor for at least twenty years. When they are younger, we should be making decisions for even longer than that. A very wise man, Roger McCarty, founder

ACTION PLAN SUMMARY
Client
Date

Complete	Action	Who	Date to be completed
Date:			
Date:			
Date:			
Date:			
Date:			
Date:			
Date:			
Date:			

ACTION PLAN SUMMARY
Bob and June Jenson
December 5, 2020

Complete	Action	Who	Date to be completed
✓ Date: 11/03/20	• Client Analysis • Initial Appointment	CFS – Amy CFS - Victoria	11/03/2020
✓ Date: 11/04/20	• Financial Objectives • Discovery Book	Mr. Jenson	11/10/2020
✓ Date: 11/17/20	• Investment Proposal • Investment Policy Statement	CFS – Victoria	11/17/2020
✓ Date: 11/30/20	• LTC Proposal • Complete Application for LTC • Life Insurance • Health Insurance	CFS – Victoria CFS - Amy	11/30/2020
✓ Date: 12/02/20	• Client Advisory Agreement • Account Set-Up	CFS - Amy	12/30/2020
✓ Date: 01/12/21	• Edward Jones – Joint ($500,600) • Edward Jones – MM ($180,000) • Edward Jones – UTMA to 529 w/ Open. ($7,500) • Edward Jones – Karen's IRA ($68,000)	CFS - Amy to set up Xfers.	01/15/2021
✓ Date:03/06/21	• 401(k) Merrill Lynch ($1,555,700)	CFS - Direct Xfer	04/2021
✓ Date:05/01/21	• Revocable Trust	Mr. Jenson	01/05/2021

and former president of Brokers International Ltd., gave me this advice almost twenty years ago: "If you wouldn't want to spend an evening having dinner with a potential client, don't take them on as a client." Another fine gentleman, Charles "Skip" Codding of the well-respected law firm of Dunlap Codding & Rogers, has shared with me on several occasions that the hardest advice to grasp for young business professionals is: "Know when to pass on business. Not all business is good business." If I do not believe that the client, my family, my company, and I would all benefit from the relationship long-term, I have no problem recommending another advisor. We cannot, nor want, to be everything to everyone. Still, we want to be everything to those we take on as clients.

Our specialty is with the affluent. Affluence is described not just in assets we manage but also in net worth—the amount of asset value exceeding total liabilities. My entire full-time focus is on their special needs. Is this going to be a good long-term relationship for all parties? If we both agree, then the answer is yes, and we move on to the next stage.

Proposal and Investment Policy Statement

After a clear picture of your financial position emerges, and your goals and tolerance for risk are determined, a proposal for the portfolio strategist is prepared along with an investment policy statement (IPS). (This is a written statement based on your risk/return profile that is a basis for all current and future investment decisions.) The next step is that of implementing your plan with the selections of the portfolio strategist.

Your advisor's staff, an application/implementation administrator, or another trained professional should be responsible for processing all paperwork required. If needed, you should assist these professionals as they follow through until all accounts have been set up. Remember, they are working *on your behalf* with all parties concerned, including custodian, the reporting companies, money management, and whomever else may be affected.

Then there's a final review for accuracy before the presentation to you; this is just a commonsense approach to put everything on paper for your benefit as well as the benefit of the advisor.

Initial 45-Day Review

After we've established your investment account, we'll meet again to review strategy and provide you with your ID and password for our secure Online Account Center.

Reporting and Monitoring

Each quarter, we deliver a comprehensive Quarterly Performance Review showing you exactly where you are in relation to your goals, objectives, risk tolerance, etc. When, and if, your financial circumstances change, we'll be ready to suggest changes to your investment strategy. With this approach, you, as the client, have the security of flexibility to make necessary adjustments with the stroke of a pen—thus eliminating the tax issues, fees, and expenses.

Duties and Responsibilities of Investors as Well as Advisors

As I have shared previously, advisors have fiduciary responsibilities to their clients. So what about the investor? Any reputable advisor will discuss with you in detail what your responsibilities are as a client and investor. As your trusted advisor, we can only give you our best recommendations when we have all the information we request. You must provide us with all relevant information on your financial condition, net worth, risk tolerance, job status, family situation, health, etc., and you must notify us promptly of any changes in this information. You should also read and understand the information provided by your advisor.

Here is one of my favorite examples. A couple, who have been clients for several years, asked my advice about real estate investing. We discussed their options of investing in a mutual fund real estate investment trust (REIT) or purchasing rental properties. They are both top executives with demanding careers, in addition to two young daughters and elderly parents. Their time was very limited. I suggested considering a REIT mutual fund rather than rental property. Being a landlord is very time consuming and not for everybody. After our meeting, I spent the next several months researching different REITs that I believed would be appropriate for their needs. At the next meeting, I expressed some concern that the value of one of their money market accounts that usually had a minimum balance of $100,000 had dropped considerably. Before this, I had sent them information to review on a specific real estate mutual fund and had not heard from them regarding any questions. When asked about the decline, they looked at each other, and the wife said, "Oh, that $100,000 account is the account we used for the down payments for the two investment properties."

I said, "Really, when did you buy investment property?"

They replied, "Several months ago, I guess we should have called and told you."

Now remember, I am their trusted advisor. They have a responsibility to inform me of any changes, including withdrawing money from an account we agreed would maintain a $100,000 balance. As you can imagine, my first concern was the potential of identity theft. I shared with them that, as their advisor, I spent many hours researching REITs based on our last conversation.

The wife said, "You know, I just still have a difficult time remembering to let you know about changes and decisions we make. The only time we heard from our previous advisor was when he wanted to sell us something."

The ChappelWood model offers a different and much healthier relationship. We work for our clients. We do not spend our days looking for things to sell. We seek out solutions and opportunities.

The Unreasonable Client

There is such a thing as an unreasonable client. It's a person who has unreasonable expectations. A young man called my office and told my assistant he wanted me to take over their company's

401(k) plan. I returned his call and asked how he'd heard about us, and he said he heard me on the radio. He seemed like a bright and delightful young man. I asked for a copy of his current statement as well as information about his third-party administrator (TPA). (This is usually a CPA who administers the plan.) He asked why I would need to know that since he just wanted an appointment and then have me take over their plan. I told him it was simple; I didn't want to waste his time or mine. I needed to know the reason he wanted to replace his investment advisor. I wanted to know if the dissatisfaction was due to the investment advisor, their investment selection, the third-party administrator, or his company being unreasonable.

Keep in mind this was a substantial account that typically anyone would have jumped on immediately. At ChappelWood, we have a policy of under promising and over delivering; we don't ever want to commit to a promise we know we cannot keep just for the money, honey!

He just chuckled and sent the information over to my office that afternoon for my review. I was delighted to know after a quick review that the problem was simply that they were paying for services they were not getting. That was easy enough to solve. We provided the company competent professionals and a good mutual fund company with a long history of solid performance and investment workbooks that would help their employees.

Identifying the problem helps me to create the solutions. The implementation is the challenge. Thank goodness for competent, great back-office support. Another case involved a man with a substantial portfolio. He contacted me after years of reading about me, listening to me on the radio, and hearing people say I was a conservative advisor—that really means prudent. He had lost a substantial amount of his portfolio in 2000 and would give me all his money to manage *if* I could get him a 50 percent return every year over the next five years. Bottom line: he wanted me to fix his mistake! This was not a person who could convince me that consistency isn't the most reliable philosophy. I actually liked this gentleman; however, I seriously couldn't comply with such an unreasonable request. I politely told him he would have to go elsewhere and pointed toward the door. We don't make promises we can't keep just to get additional assets under management. Eventually, we agreed to compromise on more realistic goals and objectives.

It's easy for me to send potential clients on their way because I have the privilege of selecting the clients I enjoy working with. It is every advisor's dream. I have long since stopped taking on any new client who "fogs a mirror"—a commonly used phrase in the financial services industry for rookies who take just about anyone as a client.

THE DIVA'S ADVICE

1. An advisor from an independent background most likely will bring a fresh perspective to your portfolio that many in the larger wire houses can't.

2. The ChappelWood business model is a model I recommend you use when looking to hire someone for financial advice. Are you getting through to the advisor quickly when calling? Are you receiving easy-to-understand statements? Ask for a sample copy. If not, keep looking for someone to hire.

3. The initial client process requires a sharing of information. Don't be alarmed. Any true professional who values their time, as well as yours, will ask for information. This allows the advisor to know objectives, goals, and status of a potential client. It also provides a road map on getting from Point A to Point B of an investment or retirement goal.

4. A dear friend of mine, Lea Black from Miami, Florida—a dynamic woman and known for her "fund-raising prowess,"—told me years ago, "people will spend their money and time on what they place most value." Your financial advisor should learn what your priorities and values are and help you to achieve them.

5. An Investment policy statement (IPS) should include:
   - Time horizon
   - Risk tolerance
   - Investment objectives
   - Asset allocation
   - Rebalancing procedures
   - Investment (Asset classes)
   - Liquidity
   - Duties and responsibilities

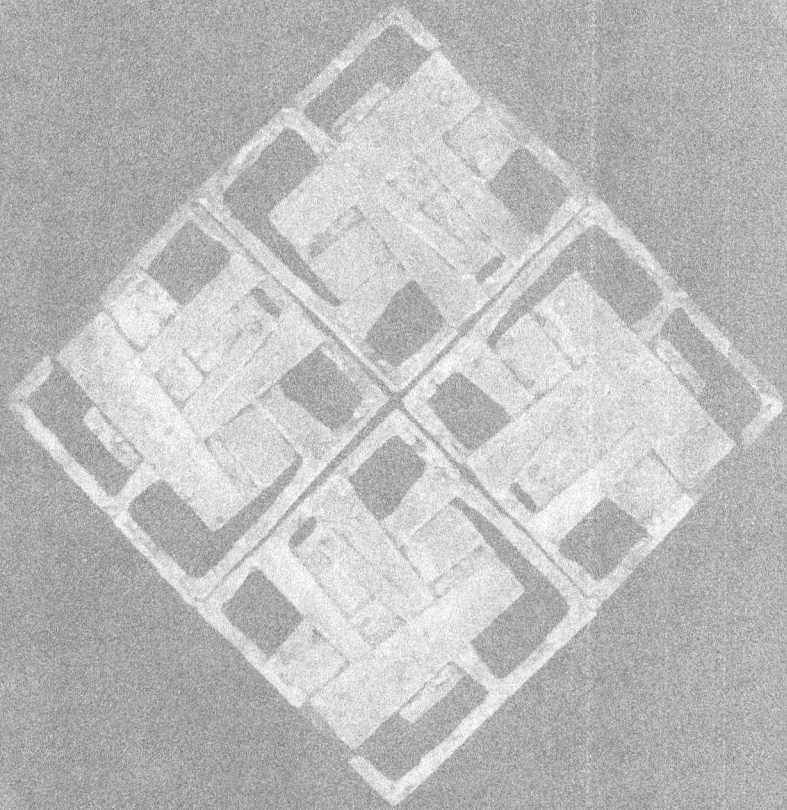

CHAPTER 6

Aspects of Financial Planning: Rollovers, Retirement, and Inheritance

It's not what you earn but what you keep.
—Diva

Why do I specialize in inheritances? When a person or family receives an inheritance, many times they don't have more than $400 in the bank, or the individual lost a spouse through death or divorce and did not handle the family's finances. In other words, they have little savvy when it comes to money, and they need an advisor who will take the time to guide them through this new minefield. Dave Ramsey, a debt counselor and financial columnist, has referred to me many times as having "the heart of a teacher."

My high school English teacher, Ms. Collins, would have loved to have heard that. She asked me to stay after class one day during my junior year and told me I should consider being a teacher. Back then I thought she was crazy. I realize she was a very smart lady, as I have since made a career of teaching and sharing.

When it comes to planning, most advisors won't ask how much of your inheritance you plan to give away. At ChappelWood Financial Services, it's a consideration. Remember, "It's All About The $Money, Honey!®" Most advisors I have heard don't even consider the question of your giving. Why? Because the more money they invest for you, the more money they earn. If your advisor asks about giving some of the inheritance, I will tend to believe he or she has integrity.

Most people claim they would give away ten percent of an inheritance or lottery winnings. Let's say you received a $1 million inheritance. Would you *really* give away $100,000? I remember one client who donated a full ten percent. To this day, if you asked her if that was the right decision, you only have to look at the glow on her face to know the answer. She only once mentioned to me some of the money she donated and gave away. I can't remember the specifics, however I will always have the memory of the glow and smile as she described her giving. By the way, she has never had that look when she has had an incredibly good performance review!

Being a good steward of your money means giving to worthy causes. God loves a cheerful giver (2 Corinthians 9:7). My belief is that almost any "giving" is a worthy cause. It may be donated to help a friend or family member in need. Maybe it's for a child who does not have the means to attend college or a great teacher who is in dire need of school supplies. The list can also include the institute of higher education that provided your education or groups that help the homeless or abused women. You see, there are so many worthy causes. It's your money, honey, so you get to decide! How exciting is that?

When someone comes to me with an inheritance, I have an initial consultation, finding out as much as I can and sharing about our processes and how I can assist them. Then I surprise them by giving them this advice: "I encourage you to interview a bank and a wire house now that you know our process and services. It will allow you to compare and select the right relationship for you."

You see, I have no fear. We are not a car dealership. If it's good for you today, it will be good for you tomorrow or next week. You are making a long-term decision. This is not a one time sale. I want a potential client to know what a unique experience we provide at ChappelWood Financial Services. If they come to us first and then have appointments with a bank and a wire house, they will see for themselves the difference. They will truly appreciate the unique experience we offer. I recommend that you do the same. Go in armed with knowledge and with confidence.

Rollovers

What would you think is the most commonly asked question on my radio show? "Victoria, I have a 401(k) at a previous employer. Should I leave it there, or roll it into my current employer's plan?" The simple answer is neither. You should roll your 401(k) plan into a self-directed IRA. Here are the reasons:

1. Your employer typically has limited options when establishing a 401(k) that may not always meet your particular objectives, needs, and suitability.

2. With a self-directed IRA, you have all the choices available in the marketplace.

3. Furthermore, if you leave your money in a 401(k) and your company makes a change in a fund company, many times your money will simply be allocated to a cash management/money market. That account may not earn enough interest to keep up with inflation.

There is a big misconception about the simplicity on this subject. One of my favorite books is *The World is Flat* by Thomas Friedman[7], an excellent writer and researcher. Friedman has made a career writing for such prestigious newspapers as the *New York Times* and *Washington Post*. Monica Shine, who enjoyed this book, sent it to me as an early birthday gift. I loved it. It was fascinating and

---

7 Thomas Friedman, *The World is Flat: A Brief History of the Twenty-First Century.* (Farrar, Strauss, and Giroux, April 5, 2005).

informative. Towards the end of the book, Friedman referred to a subject that I don't believe he knows a thing about. He lost some credibility with me.

He explained[8] how difficult it was to roll over your 401(k) to a self-directed IRA, which you control. Nothing could be further from the truth. First, a rollover means a tax-free transfer of funds from one retirement plan to another. Let's go to a sports analogy for an illustration.

Visualize a football game. As the action gets under way, the quarterback calls the play. He takes the snap, stands, and plants his feet as his receiver runs down the field. He spots his receiver and spirals the football (your 401(k) funds) down the field. The receiver, new custodian of your 401(k), catches the ball for the perfect play. Does that sound complicated to you? Of course not. Still, it behooves you to have a financial advisor who will provide a client analysis, risk tolerance profile, goals, and objectives for you. In order to recommend the most suitable investments, be sure the account is set up correctly and verifies the transfer is tax free. That is another reason you hire an advisor to execute the transfer— Greeks talking to Greeks.

Retirement Planning

The most important thing to know about retirement planning is that there is no "one size fits all." Every client is different. Clients have different family issues and different wants and needs. For example, I have clients that don't want to leave any money to their children. They just want to spend it all until there is exactly a zero balance in their accounts on the day they die. The No. 1 priority of others is to leave a large inheritance to their children.

A large majority of my clients want to leave a legacy to their church, a foundation, university, or other worthwhile cause. Chuck Hodges says, "It is a sin to die rich." The challenge for me is to help my clients achieve their goals regardless of what they

---

8 Friedman, The World is Flat, 285.

are. My first obligation is to determine what the goals are and how much money it will take to get them there. That may include leaving an inheritance, buying a vacation home in the mountains, or being on a golf course in Palm Springs. Who knows? They may want to retire early. Regardless, it's up to me to present the options, solutions, and probabilities. Even though there is no "one size fits all," there are some basic steps and understanding each investor should have.

There are three phases of financial planning throughout your life: accumulation, capital preservation, and finally, distribution to heirs and charities. From the moment we are born, we start "accumulating" stuff (even before we are born, thanks to family and friends)—homes, cars, businesses, investment portfolios, real estate, etc. As we accumulate, there comes a point we say stop! We are now more concerned with the "preservation" of what we have accumulated than growth. In other words, there comes a point that we take a more conservative, less risk approach to the management of our Investment Portfolio. We become more concerned about the return of our money than the return on our money. Typically, this happens close to when the average investor is considering retirement.

You now own your own time; you are financially independent; you have traveled everywhere you wanted to go, played all the golf, surfed every ocean, and sailed every sea. In other words, you have done and bought everything that is a part of a happy, abundant existence, and now you are more concerned with your "distribution" of your assets to heirs and charities—in my office we refer to this as the client's social legacy.

Now the question is, how do you want to be remembered? What charitable organizations do you want to continue to contribute to long after you have passed on? Most of my clients are very charitable. There are organizations and institutions they believed in and want to continue to support, such as the university that gave them their education and advantage to be successful.

Retirement and Capital Preservation

For years I couldn't understand why the industry's philosophy was to put all assets in stocks and bonds, and then when a person retired, take dividend income off the whole account. The market can take a dramatic drop, and sadly you have set yourself up for disaster. I have always been a commonsense type of girl. It seems to me, the most commonsense thing to do is use this three-step approach that has worked quite well—provided you have not already created a problem for yourself—and to this date, a client has never run out of money.

Investment Mistakes

There are three common mistakes I see investors make when they come to me for advice.

1. They have not planned for different scenarios, such as early retirement before the age of fifty-nine-and-a-half.
2. They have all their assets in stocks and a few bonds. As mentioned earlier, a dramatic drop in the market can send those plans on the same path as the cruise liner, Titanic. The Diva firmly recommends you always avoid financial icebergs.
3. They have not properly protected their assets from major health issues, or not taken the proper steps to pass their assets on to their heirs. At a minimum, they need long-term care insurance and living revocable trusts (see the retirement planning checklist on page 88.)

THE DIVA'S ADVICE

1. What you don't know about inheritances could cost you dearly. Shop around. A private independent financial company can provide the service and analysis to assist you in clarifying, organizing, and simplifying the financial part of your life.

2. For retirements, one size does not fit all. Clients have various goals as well as many options and ways to get there. Your advisor should help you clarify and achieve your goals.

3. Your 401(k) plan can be a substantial part of your retirement plan. If some tell you it's difficult to transfer that plan to a self-directed IRA, don't believe them. It's done every day.

4. There are common mistakes investors make. Be careful and plan for the unexpected. The bottom line could be hundreds of thousands of dollars lost, if not your entire portfolio.

RETIREMENT PLANNING CHECKLIST

Clarifying, Organizing, and Simplifying the financial part of your life.

When preparing for Retirement Day, you should start the process at least 36 months in advance..

36 Months Prior to Retirement

	Request a written copy of your employer's qualified plan and distribution options and research your company's benefits policy for retirees.
	Review any debt you hold. Do not go into retirement with debt.
	Determine a living expense budget for retirement. If you don't currently have an Investment Advisor, start interviewing immediately. If your primary investable asset is your employer retirement plan, expect to pay an hourly advisory fee or a percentage fee based on the value of your 401(k), 403(b), TSP, Pension, ESOP, or value of your business.
	Develop an Investment Policy Statement (IPS)—your Investment Advisor can assist with this.
	Provide your Investment Advisor with contact information for your advisory team which should consist of a CPA, Tax Attorney, and Trust Attorney at minimum.
	Develop an Action Plan with your Investment Advisor for your Advisory Team.

12 Months Prior to Retirement

	Request company retirement forms which are also known are Distribution Forms.
	Look into Life and Health Insurance options, including Long Term Care, if your benefits are not portable from your company.
	Establish your IRA Rollover account with your Investment Advisor 30 to 60 days prior to your retirement date to ensure a smooth monetary transaction.
	Your advisor's implementation team should review all of your company's rollover paperwork and submit it to the appropriate persons within your company 30 days (or a specified date) prior to your effective retirement date. The implementation team should also conduct the monetary transfer on your behalf to ensure prior taxation or lack thereof is conducted.

> "
> The most important thing to know about retirement planning is that there is no 'one size fits all.' Every client is different.
> "

1. Victoria at her first edition book premiere.

2. Victoria and her husband Larry.

3. Diva Champagne with Dennis Jaggi, and Victoria.

4. Wallace Johnson, Victoria, and JoAnn Johnson.

5. Interviewed by Meredith Vieira on the *Today* show, during Sweeps Week.

6. Victoria receiving her Global Wealth Manager Award in Athens, Greece.

7. Guest of Chris Harrison, host of the Bachelor: *Women Tell All* and Victoria.

1. Victoria and Larry, with the children they sponsored along with Allied Arts, for *The Nutcracker*.

2. Most fun interview; Host of *Success Today* with Bachelor Bob... Bachelor Nation Fans.

3. Victoria and Governor Stitt, at the Governor's Boots and Bandannas.

4. Victoria's Executive Board, the Commission on the Status of Women.

5. Victoria sharing information regarding the Women's Hall of Fame (OWHOF) at the swearing-in ceremony with Governor Stitt.

6. On the set of *It's All About the $Money Honey!*®

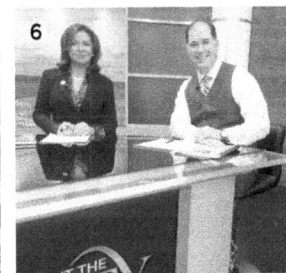

7. Host of the 4th Annual Kentucky Derby Soiree with guests Justin Avera, Harvey, Victoria, Samantha, thoroughbred, Sandy Kraft, and Governor Kevin Stitt.

1. Appearing in the Real Housewives of Miami at Red River Bar, with Lynn Fontaine, Lisa Horchstein, Eve McCandless, Victoria, Lea Haller-Black, Merrie Arnspiger and Liza Aponte.

2. Victoria and Baywatch's Pamela Anderson.

3. Victoria and President Donald Trump.

4. Toby Keith, and Victoria, 2020.

5. Rush Limbaugh and Victoria.

6. Dell Corporation's Appreciation Award for Victoria's Dell Lunch and Learn.

7. JoAnn Johnson, Victoria and Wallace Johnson, the ChappelWood Client Paris Soiree.

8. Victoria taking self-defense training in Dallas for at risk executives.

1. Lunch with *Saving Grace*'s creator, Nancy Miller, and Major General Rita Aragon.

2. Victoria and "Fuzzy" at Gaillardia Country Club.

3. Victoria with Heisman Trophy winner, Steve Owens, and others at the Charity Golf tournament.

4 Victoria in wardrobe for *Saving Grace* with Lorraine Trousant, and Major General Rita Aragon.

5. Victoria taking Elizabeth Blaise under her mentoring wings in New York.

6. Victoria selling a CMA Awards Auction item to Harold Matzner (philantropist, owner of the Tennis Club and Spencer's Restaurant in Palm Springs) at a Dusty Wings fundraiser.

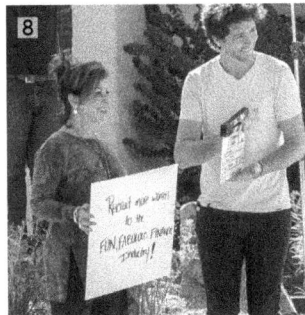

7. At the CMA Awards with Gayle Hodges, philanthropist and former owner of Prime Time International.

8. Inspiring Victoria filming a commercial in Scottsdale to motivate women to join the financial services industry.

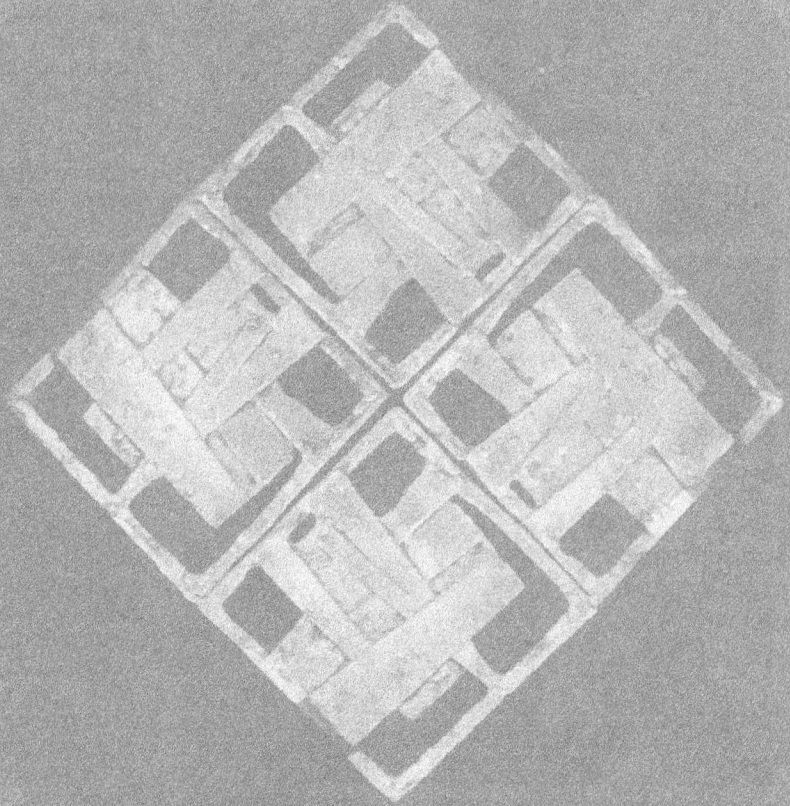

CHAPTER 7

Disciplined Investing

Consistency will always outperform
occasional brilliance.
—Diva

If you decide to lose ten pounds, could you diet for a day or just not eat for a day and accomplish the goal? Of course not! You would need to first do the following:

- Make the decision you want to lose weight.
- Determine how much weight you want to lose.
- Calculate how many weeks it will take.
- Plan a good, healthy-eating menu.
- Decide what kind of exercise you are willing to do to increase your metabolism and burn fat.
- Determine how you will maintain your weight loss.

Your Financial Plan is Very Similar. You Need to:

- Make the decision, commit, and hire an advisor.
- Determine how much you will need for retirement to live your lifestyle, not someone else's.
- Determine your social legacy.
- Calculate, based on your risk tolerance, how much you need to invest to meet your goals. For you DIYers, please access one

of many calculators on my website, FinancialDiva.com. Click ChappelWood for calculators.

- Select portfolio strategists who will assist you in meeting your goals and objectives.
- Implement your plans.
- Protect your assets.
- Monitor your plan. Do not invest and forget.

Once you have the plan in place, it takes discipline and consistency to continue to follow the plan. Many things are out of your control, such as the market, inflation, media, government, war, and many other factors. Some of these risks may make you doubt your plan. This is yet another good reason to have an advisor. The advisor can keep you on track and help determine if and when changes to the plan are necessary. When you plan properly and have confidence in your plan, you will find it only needs minor adjustments over time unless some catastrophic event takes place.

Who's an Investment Advisor?

Use caution and diligence in selecting an investment advisor. Consider background, education, experience, and partnerships. For example, where did this person come from, and can he or she appreciate how you've built your wealth on your own?

Also examine the training, licensing, and certification of any potential advisor as well as how successful he or she has been as a business owner. Has this person succeeded as an investor, business owner, real estate developer, real estate agent, or community leader?

What kind of track record does the potential advisor have where partnerships are concerned? What's the record of working with top portfolio managers? Can he or she provide the team approach to be your primary advisor?

Rebalancing

I loved the 1990s! Who didn't? It seemed like just about anyone could make money investing, right? Yes, it was proven on more than one occasion; however, it's like losing weight—it's only good if you maintain your weight loss. So many didn't. This is what I saw happen all too often. Investors and advisors put so much money in tech stocks and tech mutual funds. Many were heavily weighted towards tech, and the clients never rebalanced their portfolios for appropriate diversification; or in other words, allocating your assets over many asset classes and rebalancing. It's been proven that 91.5 percent of your success is based on diversification. Typically, this is done on a quarterly basis. Simply put, it takes a little bit of everything—smartly invested—and it takes staying in balance to keep your risk level as dictated by your Investment Policy Statement (IPS).

Once I had a client who was tempted by a risky strategy. One of her mutual funds had a 105 percent return, and she wanted to take money from core growth mutual fund accounts to reallocate them over to the fund that had a 105 percent return. My suggestion was to come by the office, and we would discuss it. Now, I am not one to want to embarrass anyone, so instead of saying, "What in the world are you thinking? You are an intelligent person!" Instead, I said, "That's an interesting idea. Let me ask you something. What do you think the odds are of this tech fund having a positive return next year if this year the return was 105 percent?" It wasn't very likely. The client answered her own question and immediately saw the risk.

I certainly would have been very impressed had this individual come to me and said, "What do you think about this ABC fund that had an eight percent return and my buying more shares? I think it is undervalued."

That's not human nature. Our nature is to chase the highest returns, which is the opposite of a disciplined long-term strategy of portfolio strategists. They don't make emotional decisions with your money. Furthermore, this client was preparing to retire in the next twelve months. Moving more dollars into the aggressive account would not have been a smart decision. In reality, what was more appropriate was to review her entire portfolio against her stated objectives and reallocate her growth in that fund account to her growth bond and value accounts. That kept her risk level at objectives stated in her IPS.

If you had tremendous returns in the 1990s in the tech market, the smart and prudent thing was to examine the risks. In our client's case, no more than ten percent of her portfolio was aggressive. Therefore, if the gains grew to fifteen percent, we would sell—not buy—the aggressive equities and purchase the more consistent fixed income or bonds. Doesn't sound too sexy, does it?

Sorry, that is why you have a trusted advisor to help you make the right decisions, sexy or not. What was smart about this investor was she called to ask her trusted advisor. Some of you may not have been that lucky in the 1990s. Many of you didn't make an informed decision, and you can chalk it up to "education is expensive"—just look at the price of tuition today. You can learn from that experience and do better from now on.

Make sure you have a written IPS and review it to be sure you are not wavering from your plan without good reason. Emotions are not good, sound reasons. This is especially true when the market starts going crazy, and I know it is difficult not to get caught up in all the emotions.

Please heed the Diva's advice here. Don't do it. Some are reallocating their 401(k)s, heavily weighting themselves in the emerging markets. The one thing I have learned is I cannot save the world. I can only take care of my little place in the universe and help those who sincerely want to help themselves.

Another nugget of advice I truly hope you take from the Diva is the Contrarian Theory. This strongly suggests going against what most of the crowd is doing. The Contrarian Theory takes the opposite position from the majority opinion to capitalize on overbought or oversold situations. This theory could have saved a lot of heartache for many during the tech crazes of the late 1990s. And, when everyone gravitates toward over-weighting the emerging markets, remember the wisdom of the Contrarian theory.

If your tech funds were increasing in value, you should have been rebalancing at least annually to keep your risk down. What many people did was to allow their portfolios to get out of balance and then they screamed like panthers when the market adjusted.

THE DIVA'S ADVICE

1. Compare your finances to a diet. A proper weight loss plan has goals and objectives and ways to meet those goals.

2. Your financial future also has a series of goals. There is a proper map to reach those objectives. If the plan is sound, put faith in it. Only minor adjustments are needed to handle situations out of your control.

3. Keep your portfolio balanced. Remember the 1990s? Tech stocks were the rage. Some investors and advisors invested too much in just one sector. The Contrarian Theory advises against the herd investing mentality.

4. Realize a fund performance will vary. A fund with a high yield one year may not equal that performance the next year. Your best bet? Call your financial advisor before committing other funds and throwing your portfolio out of balance, based on the risk.

5. Emerging markets are the latest craze for many investors. Know that foreign markets may be more volatile when it comes to political, economic, and market trends. Getting information and completing transactions can be more of a challenge. Beware. Think before you leap. A well maintained IPS with rebalancing demands consistency and discipline.

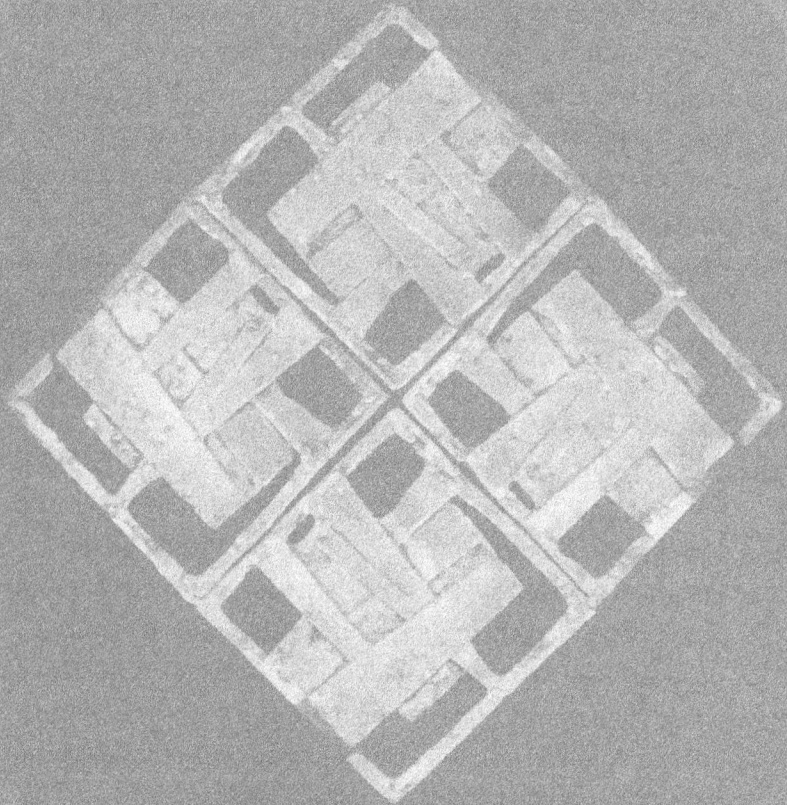

CHAPTER 8

Investment Strategies

*Those who say it cannot be done should
not interrupt those doing it.*
—Diva

"Diva, what must I know to start investing?"
What every investor must know before investing one's hard-earned dollar is, left to our devices, we will hurt our own selves. (Refer again to the Cycle of Emotion on page 125.) You most definitely need a trusted advisor.

Beyond your investment timing or the specific securities, if you know absolutely nothing else about investing, you must know that over 91 percent of your success is determined by your asset allocation. Your returns are driven by the way they are allocated in stocks, bonds, cash, and how they are rebalanced over time. Before making any kind of leap with your money, this strategy is something you want to understand. (See illustration, on page 102.)

Note the timing element in the illustration. Timing is less than two percent in determining your possibilities of success. Does good timing happen? There are those who strike oil, hit the mother lode, grab a dot com, or win the lottery—but what are the odds? Are you willing to risk your future? Those who enjoy cardiac arrest should be sure to include this high risk money in their portfolio.

ASSET ALLOCATION IS THE MOST IMPORTANT DETERMINANT OF VARIANCE IN PORTFOLIO PERFORMANCE.

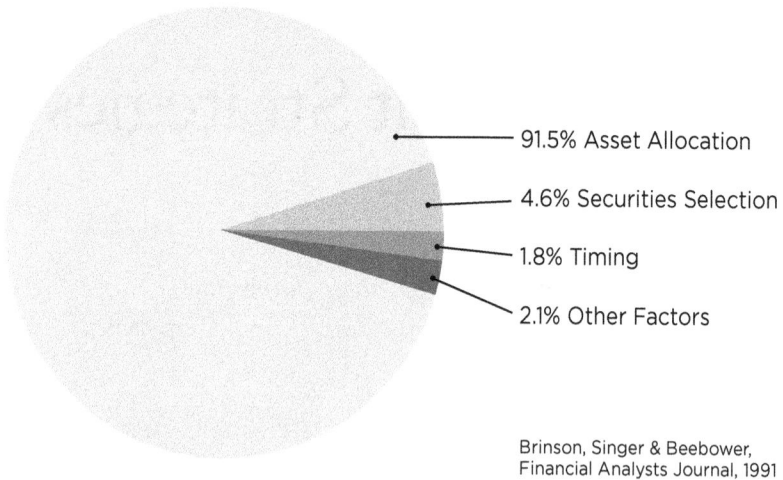

91.5% Asset Allocation

4.6% Securities Selection

1.8% Timing

2.1% Other Factors

Brinson, Singer & Beebower,
Financial Analysts Journal, 1991

Concerning investment and wealth creation, let's take a look at some of the definitions—later I'll give you my take on them.

Asset Allocation/Diversification: This investment strategy is designed to reduce the risk by spreading the risk over several industries, market sectors, or a larger number of companies. The operating assumption is that diversified investments are unlikely to all move in the same direction. This allows gains in one investment to offset the losses of another. Dare to Be Different! Remember that long-term investing requires diversification for success.

Rebalancing: Over time, market conditions and the varied performance of asset classes may cause the portfolio's asset mix to vary from the original target allocation. To remain consistent with the asset allocation guidelines established, each asset class should be reviewed periodically—typically quarterly, but at least annually—to maintain the initial target allocation established.

I don't recommend putting all your eggs in one basket. I encourage my clients in the southwest who are heavily invested in oil and gas—and my clients in California who are heavily invested in the agricultural business—to invest in other asset classes.

Four Major Types of Risk

1. Market risk, also called systematic risk, is the portion of a security's risk common to all securities in the same asset class, and the risk cannot be eliminated through diversification. For example, a market risk associated with investment in stocks is the general tendency of share prices to decrease during an economic downturn.

2. Inflation risk occurs when you invest in assets with rates of return that are too low to counter the effects of rising prices on the value of your money. Many investors are tempted to hold only "safe" assets such as short-term bonds or cash that don't fluctuate in value as much as stocks. The problem is that a portfolio consisting of bonds and cash is at the mercy of inflation (see chart on page 104). These types of assets historically have had a hard time keeping pace with rising prices. Inflation's effect on your savings can be even worse than a market meltdown. The value of $1 million today will falter around $440,000 in twenty years, assuming a modest three percent inflation rate.

3. Corporate risk, also called company specific risk, is the risk you take by owning a particular stock or other security. Individual stocks often fall due to company-specific factors, even as the market as a whole rises.

4. Legislative risk concerns new laws or regulations that may have the potential to pose a challenge for your portfolio. New taxes may also have an effect. Make sure you ask your investment advisor about tax efficiency. The manager can pursue a range of tax management strategies to address specific tax considerations.

Types of Strategies

Two of the more common strategies involve what are known as the Strategic Asset Allocation (SAA) approach and the Tactical Asset

HOW INFLATION CAN AFFECT A PLAN

You need to make a few changes in your plan.

Savings of $19,699 monthly may total $10,000,000 in 15 years.

You need to make a few changes in your plan. Current savings plan may be able to reach a savings goal of $10,000,000 in 31.4 years. Adjusted for 3.00% inflation, $10,000,000 would be worth $6,418,619 after 15 years in today's dollars.

To reach your target in 15 years, you can do one of the following:
- Change your monthly obligation to $19,699
- Receive an annual rate of return of 22.10%

Your Input Values

Savings Goal	$10,000,000
Years to Save	15
Amount Currently Saved	$500,000
Monthly Savings	$1
Expected Rate of Return	10.00%
Inflation Rate	3.00%

Savings Results by Year

Year	Contribute $1 Monthly $500,000 Starting Balance	Contribute $19,699 Monthly $500,000 Starting Balance
1	$550,013	$799,011
2	$605,027	$1,127,902
3	$685,542	$1,489,663
4	$723,108	$1,887,663
5	$806,332	$2,325,430
6	$885,878	$2,806,974
7	$974,478	$3,336,672
8	$1,071,939	$3,919,341
9	$1,179,145	$4,500,276
10	$1,297,073	$5,265,304
11	$1,426,793	$6,040,835
12	$1,569,484	$6,893,920
13	$1,726,448	$7,832,313
14	$1,899,103	$8,864,545
15	$2,089,026	$10,000,000

Allocation (TAA) approach. I invite you to see our glossary for a complete definition of both terms. Your trusted advisor will be able to explain them fully as well. They are vital for you to understand before entering the world of investing. In brief, the Strategic Asset Allocation approach is generally considered more conservative as investments are spread over different stocks and bonds. These investments historically have solid and modest returns. The Tactical Asset Allocation approach is normally seen as a more active strategy with some emphasis on short-term profits.

It's easier to grasp the concepts if you can picture two airlines planning a flight to New York on the same day. Both airlines and pilots are concerned about a heavy thunderstorm between the departure point and New York. The first pilot has confidence in his seat belts, jetliner, instruments, and crew and will plow on to the "Big Apple" despite the ups and downs of the storm—he is fixed on the original flight plan. Pilot No. 2 decides to make adjustments to his flight plan and diverts the flight, going over or around the storm. In the end, both pilots arrive at the same destination using different strategies to achieve the same goal. The first pilot has used a more Strategic Approach while the second pilot used a more Tactical Approach.

Golf Course Bragging Rights

No look at investing would be complete without talking about a subject the Diva coined, "Golf Course Bragging Rights." If you know anything about golf, you may already know what I'm talking about.

On golf courses everywhere, there is more at stake than deciding on which iron to use to clear the sand trap and reach the green. Golfers tackle a whole array of topics while on the course. World problems are solved, and business deals are sealed. Occasionally, someone will hit a good shot.

Somewhere between teeing off and reaching the clubhouse, golf course bragging rights are on the line. A dear client of mine,

Del, is a good example. One of Del's golf buddies, who had gone to college with him, had been his advisor. You can bet Del didn't ask him the series of questions outlined in chapter four when selecting a trusted advisor.

When they got together, investment talk centered on percentages. The higher the percentage, the better off the golfer felt. One fund had returned 36 percent, and another returned a whopping 106 percent.

The talk about high percentages doesn't really talk about the real nuts and bolts of investing: the money. How much money is the investor getting back? Is it $20,000 or $2 million?

When Del and I finally met, he admitted he was impressed with my conservative thinking. This had everything to do with the way I recommend investing in the market and not my political beliefs. I believe in steady market performers and portfolio strategists with good track records. Del picked up on my philosophy.

"Victoria, what I like about you is that it doesn't matter if it's $50,000, $500,000 or $5 million, you treat it like it's real money." That's because it is.

Del faced one last problem. How could he still maintain "Golf Course Bragging Rights?" Under my plan, his returns could be consistent; however, that's not what would impress Del's circle of golf buddies. I offered a simple solution: brag about the portion of his portfolio that had the highest return, not the return for the entire portfolio. That got the job done!

"Not in a Million Years"

While discussing investing, I would be remiss if I didn't mention the story of Antonia. She is a bright, young woman I met while taking a continuing financial education class in Dallas. She impressed me with her intelligence and wit. I was a bit perplexed when she called me and told me about a possible client. This gentleman wanted Antonia to handle investments for his $5 million portfolio. Naturally, she was excited and had a 40-minute cell phone conversation with me. She wanted to go through a money manager in Texas to handle this task.

She had obviously done her homework and due diligence on the matter. Still, one money manager to handle the $5 million portfolio? My advice stunned her: "Not in a million years."

This goes back to my theory of not putting all your eggs in one basket. While the money manager in Texas may have been able to handle a portion of it, I personally would bring others in to help grow the client's investments. If this client were looking to return high yields from the Hong Kong market, doesn't it make sense to have representatives involved on the front lines in Hong Kong or New York? Diversity in investing is a must.

When One Size Does Not Fit All

In the summer of 2001, I was sitting in my temporary office building. I had sold my first office building for a large return after only thirty-six months. It was a bank I had remodeled, and I had planned on staying there for the duration of my career. It was the perfect location on a main street with regulations concerning outside signs that had been grandfathered in when I bought the building. Yet I would have been foolish not to sell when an offer for the building got extremely high. I was kind of forced into selling—every client and investor should know there is a "time to take cash."

Not wanting to pay capital gains tax, sell my business, or retire, I chose to do a 1031 exchange (see Glossary) and then acquired a two-and-a-half-acre site, which I got rezoned commercial. The construction site included a beautiful new office to call home. While the new main building was being constructed, my staff and I temporarily worked in a remodeled 1,500-square-foot building, which was previously the original homestead. It was actually perfect. This move also gave me an opportunity to review statements and portfolios since it coincided with a sharp downturn in the market.

Boxes and files literally lined up on the floor around the baseboard of my office with no more room on my credenza or desk for any more new client files. Many people were calling, trying to get in to see me. It was crazy! I was booked for weeks in advance and was working from 7:30 a.m. to eight or nine every night except for Sunday. It was not possible for me to do anymore.

I told my assistant to inform people we were doing the best we could, and if they couldn't wait their turn for a review, I would understand. They could pick up their statements from my office at any time and get a review elsewhere. That never happened. I did refuse to take one man as a client until I met his wife because he became a little testy about how long it took to see me. He and I are now the dearest of friends.

In these reviews of statements, I saw some of the oddest things. One couple, Roberta and Charles, came to me because they thought their retirement accounts might have been too aggressive for a retired couple who were in their 70s. It only took five minutes of a review to determine they were right. Every account was listed on their statement as aggressive, aggressive, and very aggressive!

The most important part of our business is making suitable recommendations for clients based on their age, health, goals, and objectives, as well as risk tolerance—the list goes on. Their investment map was clearly not appropriate for them. Being the bearer of bad news, I actually could not hold back the tears. Their portfolio needed a major overhaul. Still, I insisted they go home and discuss this in the privacy of their own home. This is certainly not the first time I had seen this type of recklessness; however, this couple was so nice and didn't deserve the poor advice that they had received.

The key to investing is finding an advisor you can trust. The advisor role, particularly in investing, is a long-term partnership—I can't emphasize this enough. An advisor works with the client and establishes financial goals and works in conjunction with the accountants and attorneys to make these goals a reality. *Make sure you have the right advisor.* That is advice you can literally take to the bank.

THE DIVA'S ADVICE

1. Make sure your strategy for investing is sound. If not, it can cost you dearly.

2. Two of the keys for the wise investor include diversification and rebalancing.

3. Don't put all your eggs in one basket. If you're heavily involved in real estate, consider other sectors for your investments.

4. All investors face risks. Those risks include market factors, inflation, corporate structure, and new laws or taxes by a government body. Remember, Uncle Sam is a partner in every business dealing.

5. Investment techniques come in strategic and tactical approaches. How aggressive or how cautious do you want to be? After all, it's your money.

6. Percentage yields on an investment may sound impressive, but how does that translate into dollars? A high return on one stock may impress your golf buddies. Still, the question you need to ask is what's the overall health of the portfolio?

7. Diversity should apply to your investment team as well. You're better served with a variety of experts in different markets.

8. One size does not fit all when it comes to investing. A couple well into retirement will face different needs than a young, corporate ladder climber looking to build his/her multi-million-dollar portfolio.

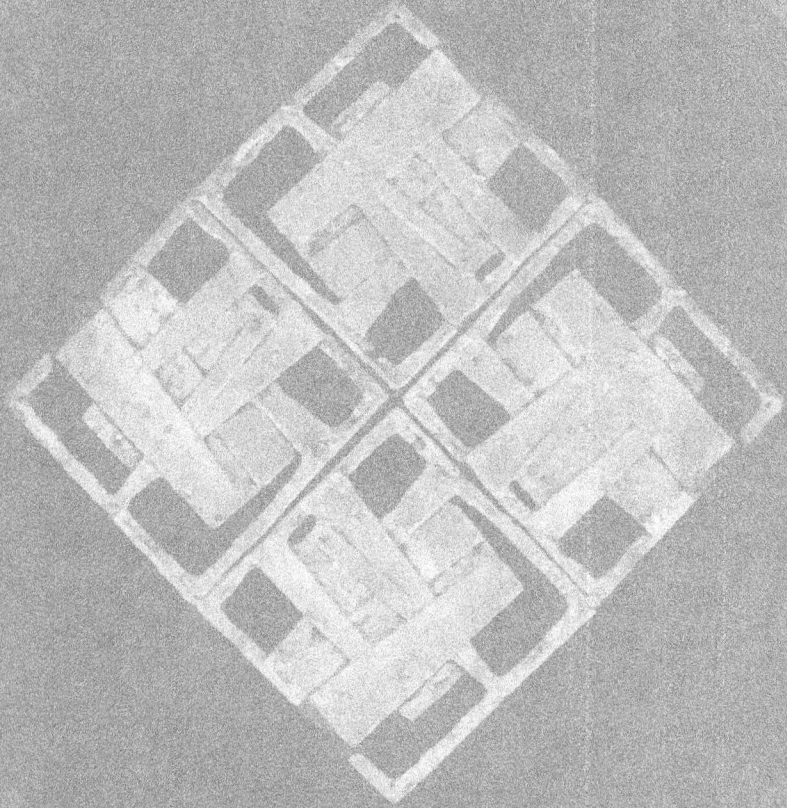

CHAPTER 9

Real Estate

The Perfect Bull's-Eye
—Diva

Both on my radio show and in my office, I am often asked advice about investing in real estate. The simple reason is because I have been very successful with all my real estate investments. Some have been profitable; some have been home runs, and one was a "perfect bull's-eye."

Know When to Hold Them, When to Fold Them, and When to Take the Cash!

Have I mentioned I am lucky? I'll let you be the judge. If you've ever read *How Successful People Win* by Ben Stein, you will remember his quote about lucky people: "Spending time with lucky, successful people, we feel lucky and successful ourselves … Something about that luck rubs off." (p. 80) He goes on to say, "The rational view is that people who give the impression of being lucky by reason of their superior training, readiness, and ability leads you into habits of competence that make you look lucky."

Some say it is my persistency, while others say it is my strong work ethic. Yet others say it is my constant pursuit of excellence. Whatever it is, I still say, "I am just lucky." Allow me to illustrate.

My first office was a back spare bedroom in my home—a smart move and the right price. Eventually, I took over the kitchen, dining room, and den. After much insistence from my husband and my CPA, I was kicked to the curb to find appropriate professional office space. I found office space; however, I was squeezed out due to the expansion of the anchor tenant. Plans were in place for me to have my own building, which I chose to give up for survivors of the 1995 Oklahoma City bombing.

Being dislocated a third time, I was starting to get a complex. I found a little bank building and negotiated a really good deal—you know it's a good deal when the broker is embarrassed to make the offer to the seller. It was one of the few times I know that I didn't leave any money on the table. From the day I bought the building, it seems there wasn't a week that didn't go by that somebody didn't say to me, "Oh, you're the lady who bought that bank building I was going to buy."

I would always say, "Oh, really." What I wanted to say was, "Yeah, if you and everybody else were going to buy it, why didn't you?" Sometimes you have to fish or cut bait. A paid-off house I owned (100 percent equity) was used for the down payment instead of out-of-pocket cash. The lender was requiring flood insurance. I had paid off three homes in five years with this same lender and never needed flood insurance before. Yet all of a sudden, the same bank decided they needed it—later I found out that one of the bank board members really wanted this building—just a coincidence? You'll never convince me.

I got some great advice from the listing agent when I asked to move the closing date. The listing agent encouraged me to do whatever it took to close because she had several offers, and one was for cash within twenty-four hours if I didn't meet the closing date. Now was that a sales pitch? One would think so until the day I closed. By then, people came out of the woodwork. They were all just about ready to close on the property themselves. A lot of them were mad that *they* hadn't finalized the deal—or so they said. Whatever the reason they didn't, I'm really glad I did, jumping through the hoops that made it happen.

After moving in and doing some minor remodeling to update the interior, I found myself making plans to expand the building by 2,000 square feet, which would almost double its size. My plans were to also lease space to a CPA and a trust attorney. Then, more elements fell into place for what some would later be regarded as the perfect bull's-eye.

It started when I attended an economic development event for the community. A gentleman—a complete stranger—sat down next to me. After some discussion, he shared about a project involving his company. I couldn't visualize exactly where it was, I just knew it was somewhere close to my building. I asked him to draw me a picture, so using a yellow legal pad, he sketched it out. The project was just north and west of my building, and it was huge—more than forty acres.

I decided to postpone my expansion until I had a better idea of what was planned. I needed to know exactly how this might positively or negatively impact my building. I watched and listened for months. The reports would vary. One moment the proposed development would impact me, and then later it wouldn't. It was going to be an apartment complex, then a theater, then a Barnes & Noble, then a Bed Bath & Beyond, and then a Super Target. The possibilities continued. I was patient and just listened and watched until all the land around me was bought up and the trees leveled.

I remember the day I pulled into my parking lot and in front of me was a red dirt lot (in Oklahoma our dirt is red—yes red) that looked like the planet Mars. It was such an ugly site. Still, I didn't want to sell my building, and I didn't want to move. I loved my building. It was a great place for my staff, my clients, and me. Even men commented on the pleasant atmosphere—which is rare for that gender to notice. And yet, plans for development in the area continued.

An acquaintance of mine finally told me I was nothing but a minor aggravation to them and should sell before they built all around me and I couldn't sell my building. He offered good advice. The only downside was that I didn't want to sell my building. Still, everyone had advice for me. If I had acted hastily, I would have been the loser. I only asked for advice from different developers and bankers I respected, and fortunately I did not take their advice.

The day I decided to sell came on a January winter's day. I drove near my building after taking a business associate to the airport. I parked across the street and thought about my situation realistically. My building was perched high on a hill, and some referred to my office as "Queen Victoria's castle." Then it dawned on me. This was not the same place I had bought. I wanted to spend the rest of my career there. Now, development had changed those plans. My building had been surrounded by beautiful trees and hills. Now that was gone.

It was that simple, and it was time to negotiate. Progress had won. Much happened during the negotiations that was funny as well as maddening for both parties. After a year of negotiations, I made up my mind that I was not going into the next year with this hanging over my head. I had a business to manage, clients to take care of, and this had become a nuisance.

It was time to "fish or cut bait." I cut the deal, believing I was leaving money on the table. Through this, I learned about "special considerations." The bottom line is that I managed to turn a piece of property I purchased for $110,000 into almost $1,000,000 in thirty-six months, and in the process messed up the skews for every realtor in town. Some might just say I was lucky. I *was* lucky to purchase the property when I did, although the rest of the story has little to do with luck. I invested a great deal of time with a lot of patience into negotiations that made this deal happen. Yet, I will confess that having a stranger sit down next to me at a conference and asking him a simple question might truly have been a stroke of good fortune.

Not too long ago, I had the opportunity to visit with the president of that development company. I reminded him that I still believed I had left at least $100,000 on the table. He let out a laugh as loud as I had ever heard and said, "Victoria, it's good to know you have a sense of humor. You hit the perfect bull's-eye!"

"What do you mean?" I said with great curiosity.

He answered, "You were up at the top end of the deal to make the numbers not work, however just under enough that they couldn't afford not to pay you."—So maybe I'm wrong. We will never know.

One of the hardest lessons I've had to learn is not that what you put out comes back (for me that is a given). Rather, I learned that good does not necessarily come back to you from the same direction as all the good you put out. In other words, you invest in one area but may be blessed abundantly in another.

What You Need to Know about Real Estate (This Can Save You Thousands of Dollars)

I may not be able to help you turn such a handsome profit on your next real estate deal; however, there are some commonsense tips you should follow when negotiating for property. To begin, find a realtor who specializes in the kind of property you want. If one realtor usually sells $1 million homes, it's almost a given that he or she will not be as up to date on the smaller markets. Next, get referrals from the realtors. They shouldn't be concerned when you ask—it's just good business. Also, talk to some of their previous customers and ask about the realtor's professionalism. Another important point: if you're selling, ask realtors how long they usually list before closing a contract. Finally, question them about how your home or commercial property will be advertised and marketed.

This is also important: ask for a settlement statement three days before closing. If you're told it's not possible, insist on it. Go over that statement, and challenge costs you don't understand or see as unreasonable.

In my many real estate dealings, I have never seen a closing statement that didn't have something that needed correcting or that I couldn't challenge. For instance, once I noticed a $350 legal fee. The attorney in question had been barred from my property, yet here was his $350 fee on the closing contract. That was not going to stand. I challenged the charge, and it was removed.

I have questioned taxes and rent credits during closing and required offices to redraft closing documents. Why? Because, in the long run, it saved me thousands of dollars. It's All About The $Money, Honey!® Make sure you ask questions before going to the closing. Most people are embarrassed to ask questions and reluctant to have documents corrected when they're sitting at the closing table. So ask for the settlement statement before the closing and question. What is the worst that can happen? You could potentially save hundreds or thousands of dollars.

A Word about Reverse Mortgages

With a lot on their mind, a couple came to me for advice. They were retired but owed $40,000 to the credit union for an equity line, which they were using to supplement their retirement income. Here was my advice to them, which I truly hope you will heed: do not go into retirement in debt. Since this couple owned their home, a reverse mortgage worked best for them. With a reverse mortgage, you still have to pay insurance and taxes on the property; however, the reverse mortgage was able to convert the couple's home equity into cash— and did it ever make a difference in their lives. Because of the reverse mortgage, the couple was able to retire the $40,000 debt and even received an extra $20,000 in cash. They were so grateful; they were in tears. These people were not my clients, but they needed help, and I was very gratified seeing them get the help they needed.

Your house is a piggy bank. You put money in. It's your money, and after sixty-two years old, you can take it out anytime you want through the reverse mortgage program. To know more, go to AARP.org.

Fifteen-Year Mortgage vs. Thirty-Year Mortgage

I'll let the following graph speak on this. I would urge you to consider taking a shorter mortgage. Why? Look at the chart below. The savings are stunning. Again, remember, it's your money, honey!

15-YEAR VS. 30-YEAR MORTGAGE *Loan Amount: $250,000* *Interest Rate: 6.50%*		
	15-Year	30-Year
Monthly Payment	$2,170.66	$1,578.75
Total Paid	$390,718	$568,350
Total Interest Paid	$140,718	$318,350
Extra Interest Paid on a 30 vs. 15		$177,632

THE DIVA'S ADVICE

1. It's deal or no deal! There's a time you decide to fish or cut bait. Timing is everything with real estate deals. When the property is worth the most, act quickly. This is another reason to have a trusted financial advisor.

2. Ask for and review the settlement statement before you go to the closing table.

3. Make sure your realtor specializes in the kind of property you wish to purchase or sell.

4. When you've found the property you want, insist on a settlement statement three days in advance. When you get it, go over it closely before signing your name to anything or going to the closing.

5. Challenge all closing costs you don't think are fair. This will most likely save you a lot of money.

6. For some who are retired, a reverse mortgage can make great sense.

7 You save a lot of money with a fifteen-year vs. a thirty-year mortgage—better yet, pay cash.

"

In my many real estate dealings,
I have never seen a closing
statement that didn't have
something that needed correcting
or that I couldn't challenge.

"

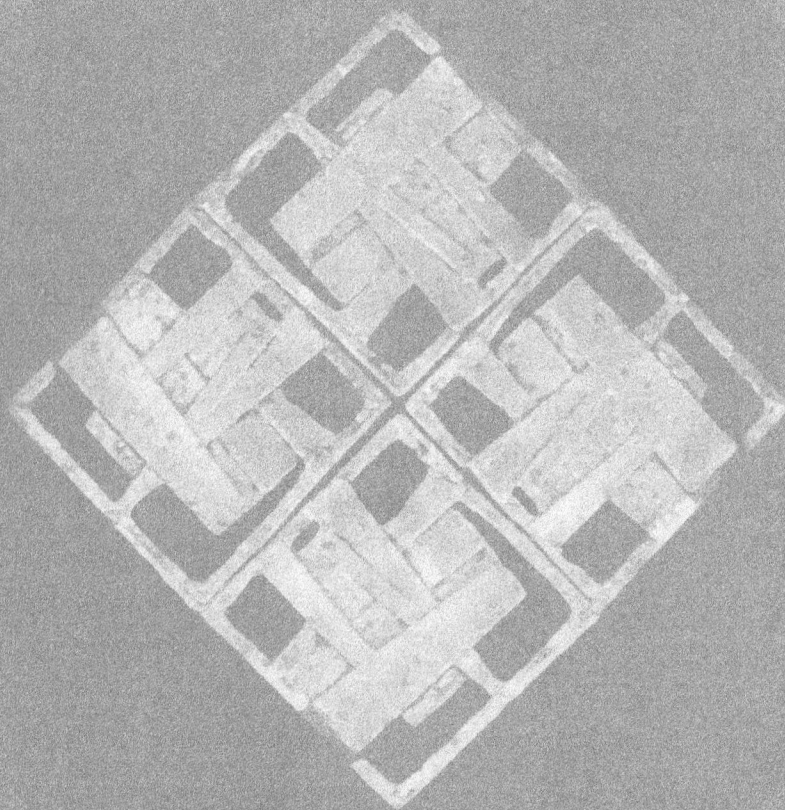

CHAPTER 10

$Money Principles

Tough Love and Paying Yourself First
—Diva

There are money principles requiring commitment and determination to avoid the follies of money mismanagement, including credit card debt. There is one action or money principle that can liberate you now. Please get a pen and discover its power. You must write down your money goals. Make a map toward wealth creation and follow it. People often tell me that they have their goals in their head. I reply, "It doesn't count unless they are written down." The power comes from writing a goal down and focusing on it every day until it is reached. Reaching goals is very simple: Step one: decide on the goal. Step two: decide what steps you can take today to get one step closer to that goal. Step three: do step two until its completion. Step four: start over at step one.

Know also that investments don't always consist of money alone. For example, your time is an investment. Achieving financial independence means you own 100 percent of your time.

Debt Works against Your Goal

Getting out of debt is really quite simple. Here are a few simple tips: First, stop spending more than you earn. If you're in a hole, stop digging it deeper. Second, write down what you earn and what you spend. And third, when you do spend, use cash! Paying with cash instead of credit gives you a much greater appreciation for the value of money.

Stop living beyond your income. Americans spend $1.20 for every dollar they earn. Anyone who has made it through third-grade math knows this spend/earn ratio is bad–very bad. Not falling for this trap is more than enough reason for you to keep reading this chapter and practice what you learn.

If you're over twelve years of age, you've had many opportunities to manage money. The odds are about 100 percent that all of us have done something that, for a lack of a better term, was stupid. This isn't being unkind; just stating the facts, so hopefully you won't take that fork in the road. Remember, education is expensive. If you have made mistakes, welcome to the club. My advice is, don't beat yourself up. Learn from your blunders and those of others and make better choices the next time. So to help you feel a little less alone, I'm going to give you some classic examples of the biggest blunders I've encountered. In my opinion, these are classic missteps. There aren't too many "happily ever after" endings for some of these people.

Creative Financing Can Create Headaches

Don't let anyone tell you that an "interest-only mortgage" is creative financing or exotic. In some rare cases, it may be appropriate; for the majority of people, though, it's reckless! Start looking for the red flags when a mortgage broker is trying to convince you to have an interest-only mortgage for a $400,000 house in Oklahoma.

In your heart, you know you qualify and should be purchasing a $250,000 home. Yet, the broker shows you a proposal where you can pay interest only, invest the rest, and pay your house off in ten years with a return on those investments. Of course, the investments he shows you have grown to more than $1 million. The problem is that most people aren't disciplined enough to invest that mortgage payment in a consistent, disciplined way. They typically spend that money to decorate their new $400,000 house, or buy a boat, a Hummer, fur coat, or jewelry.

The second problem with this type of loan is that the broker also shows you refinancing every five years to the tune of $4,000 to $5,000. Now who is making the money, Honey? It isn't you! Part of your mortgage broker's business plan is building in a guaranteed refinancing of your home every five years. It definitely doesn't take too many of these for the broker to project a nice cash flow in sixty months—I'm pretty sure his banker isn't complaining either.

Third, where is the equity in your home if you pay interest only? These are issues you need to think about before considering such a deal. I am not the only one throwing up the red flag. Others are leery as well. Former Federal Reserve chairman, Alan Greenspan, said at a banking conference that more people use interest-only loans and other techniques to buy homes they might otherwise be unable to afford. Though such loans have appropriate uses, they could also provide a way for marginally qualified buyers to borrow heavily on homes at inflated prices. Borrowers, and the institutions that service them, could be exposed to significant losses.

Horror Stories

Almost invariably, I hear about people who are investing in their 401(k), yet they have credit card debt of $10,000 to $40,000 at twelve to eighteen percent interest! (A 401(k) is a qualified retirement plan that allows eligible employees to contribute a certain amount of compensation on a pre-tax basis; earnings are tax deferred. Employers may match a stated percentage of employee contributions to the plan.)

Now don't get me wrong. Investing in your 401(k) is phenomenal—however, not when you have credit card debt. Take a moment and crunch the numbers. The market historically returns ten percent on average, yet you are paying twelve to eighteen percent credit card interest. It's easy to see who's losing on that deal—here's a hint: it's not the credit card companies.

This is not rocket science! Temporarily stop your 401(k) contribution, put all your money toward paying off the credit cards, and get back on the wealth creation track! If you have credit card debt and you have the desire to create wealth, the first and foremost thing you must do is pay off the credit card debt. This is simple. There is no exception. It's the rule—period!

It also drives me crazy when I hear stories about people who take money out of their 401(k) to pay off debts such as a car. These are tax-deferred, pre-taxed dollars, and guess what? You are penalized ten percent when you take this money out early. As a double whammy, it is also included in your income as earned income. Ouch!

A Baseball Dream That Struck Out

One of the worst stories I've ever heard regarding a 401(k) withdrawal involved a man who had a business dream and wanted my advice. He appeared intelligent, had a great job, and had $500,000 in his 401(k). He wanted to know if it was a good idea to raid this fund to start the enterprise. Naturally, I explained to him about the penalties and earned income tax issues. He was only forty, well under the fifty-nine-and-a-half minimum age for withdrawal without penalty.

He was excited about his venture. The plan was to take his $500,000 and go into business with his buddy and start a baseball card trading company. Unfortunately, no amount of explanation could convince him how reckless it was to financially kick-start his business this way. My advice was to go to every bank, every friend, and every other source he could think of before even considering touching his 401(k)! Raiding his retirement didn't make good economic sense. To be even blunter, it was reckless.

I haven't seen the man since. I can assure you if he had been successful with this business by using his 401(k), he would have made it a point to tell me, "I told you so." The 401(k) was an easy way for him to do what he wanted to do, and after all, it was his money. I'm guessing no one would lend him money for this high-risk venture. I still believe anything would have been better than taking money out of his 401(k), and I still cringe thinking about how unwise this was. He might as well have been driving down the road tossing $100 bills out the window.

THE CYCLE OF EMOTION

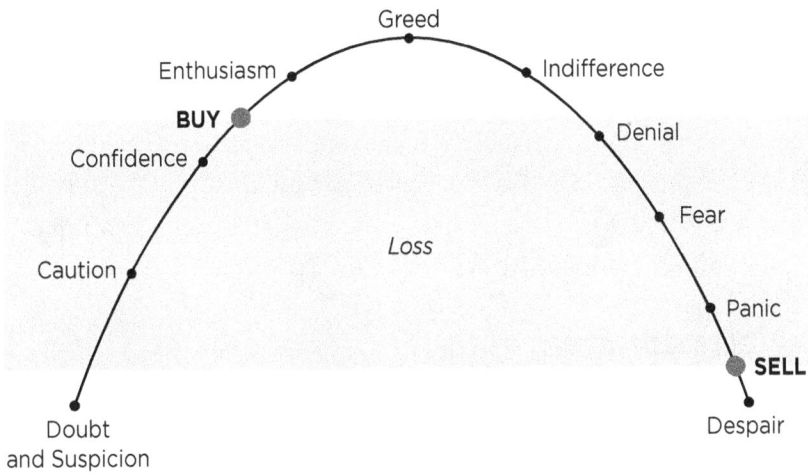

Greed

Enthusiasm · Indifference

BUY

Confidence · Denial

Caution · Fear

Loss

Panic

Doubt and Suspicion · Despair · **SELL**

Seeing Dollar Signs Instead of Common Sense

I also know intelligent people who have struggled for years and sacrificed to pay off their home. Then all of a sudden, a slick investment representative convinces them to get a mortgage on the home and invest the money in a stock or mutual fund. I once had clients who came in and asked for my advice because they had friends who were convinced by a securities broker to mortgage their house and invest in securities. Of course, their friends had been watching what I call the "emotional buying frenzy." (See Cycle of Emotion graph above.)

At first, they watched their friends' investment with skepticism. Then at the peak of the market, they decided to jump in and take out a mortgage on their paid-off home. They were retired and living comfortably when they let greed dynamite their typically good common sense. They chose to invest their mortgage money. You can pretty much guess what happened next. The market crashed shortly afterwards. They lost 75 percent of their investment and were stuck with a mortgage on their home with an 8.5 percent interest rate that they will be paying for thirty more years, and these people are sixty-five years old! Unfortunately, this isn't an isolated incident. So again, don't let greed hijack your common sense. Your momma told you, "If it sounds too good to be true, it probably is!" Once again, we're talking about being motivated by greed.

Another unfortunate case involved a young woman who had gotten some less than sage automobile advice from her father. He told her to lease a car until she decided what she wanted to buy. You do not create equity or own a vehicle when you lease it. Leasing is a misleading term that means you are renting a car! It's not an investment at all.

Bad Debt and Good Debt

Proverbs 22:7 says, "The rich rule over the poor, and the borrower is servant to the lender." My philosophy is to keep your financial strategy simple. In most instances, paying cash for your car is much smarter than leasing a car. According to the book *The Millionaire Next Door*[9], on average, wealthy people purchase vehicles two years or older, and pay cash. You say, "Oh Victoria, how can I possibly pay cash? Again, it's very simple. First, save your money and pay cash for a car you can actually afford!

You can get to work in a $4,000 car just the same as an $80,000 car. I've done both. If you don't have to pay $500 a month on a car payment, you can save the $500. Also, if you don't have to make the minimum payment of $100 to three or four credit card companies each month, you also save $400. So now you're saving $900 per month toward your next car, which will be paid in cash.

This was a lesson hard to learn for me. Yet not having a car payment on a luxury car is, well, luxurious! I remember the first time I paid cash for my car, and it was great. So can it be done? Of course it can! By the way, my first car was a baby blue Plymouth Fury II that I shared with my sister. The springs actually came out of the seats when you sat down, and it sounded like a freight train. On the plus side, I certainly wasn't in debt with the Plymouth and that was a great feeling.

---

9   Thomas J. Stanley and William D. Danko. *The Millionaire Next Door.* (Maryland: Taylor Trade Publishing, 2010).

The only exception to this rule in the Diva's world is if your car is your business. For example, if you're a realtor, you do not want to be driving around showing people $1 million homes in a $4,000 car. Investing in a nice used Infinity, Mercedes, BMW, or Cadillac is a smart move. The key word is "investing." You are investing in your livelihood and your business. That makes good sense—until you are successful enough to pay cash.

Good Debt!

Even though I am very disciplined about paying cash for everything possible, in some cases, debt can be a good investment. What you will find in this section are examples of some of my own personal experiences with good debt. This is not theory; it's real life. One form of good debt involves investing in your business. Statistics show that 96 percent of most businesses are small businesses with thirty or less employees. Our Labor Department, or Small Business Administration, classifies a small business as 500 employees or less. Yet, you only qualify for a simple IRA plan for your company if you have less than 100 employees. Is this contradictory? I guess so, but then that's our government.

Small Business Administration (SBA) loans, bank loans, venture capitalists, and combinations of all three can typically be good debt; however, a word of caution: be prepared. They are very time consuming, and there are a lot of hoops to jump through as well as plenty of paperwork to complete. Be ready also for a lot of rejection and a lot of selling, justifying, and explaining your marketing plan. Still, they are typically good loans to use in order to start or expand your own business. It's worth the time, energy, and effort. A $100,000 SBA loan can return income with profit in the second, third, fourth, or fifth year. That makes it good debt and a very shrewd investment. Patience with the paperwork is the key.

Investing in your home is also a good move. History shows that investing in your home on a fifteen-year mortgage rather than a thirty-year mortgage is the best investment (See chapter 8). Realtors will tell you, "The biggest investment you will ever make is in your home." Don't believe it! Your retirement account is the biggest financial investment you will ever make. Your home is obviously one of your larger investments. For example, I see people come in every day with a $250,000 home, yet their retirement fund is $1 million or more, and they're on target to reach $3 million to $5 million. It's pretty easy to do the math.

Credit Line! (Not to Be Confused with Credit Cards)

I am a big proponent of using credit lines for short-term money whenever possible. The two most common are: Home Equity Line of Credit (HELOC) and a Commercial Equity Line of Credit (CELOC). The benefit of using credit lines is you only use them as you need them. Therefore, you only pay interest on what you use.

Let me give you an example. Let's say you are financing a home remodeling project. Your credit line is a cool $1 million. You need $10,000 immediately to get it started, and then sixty days down the road, you need another $20,000 for the project. So at first, you're only paying interest on $10,000, and then sixty days later, you're paying on the $30,000. Then you need another $20,000 sixty days down the road. So now you have a loan of $50,000 but have staggered the interest payments. (If you know you are receiving a bonus to pay off the $50,000, an even better strategy is to wait until you receive the bonus and pay cash, thereby avoiding the interest charges.)

A commercial credit line has the same scenario; however, it is done on business projects where timing is important. For example, you believe the completed project could turn the investment into recurring revenue. You believe it is quite possible to turn $50,000 of the credit line into $100,000 in twelve to eighteen months. That is good debt because you take the $50,000 to pay off your loan and have $50,000 in revenue profit to reinvest, much like reinvesting your dividends and capital gains. So now, you are financing yourself. In other words, you're the banker for your next project, which is a great scenario. You no longer need an SBA loan, a bank loan, or a venture capitalist. Remember, these loans are time-consuming, and time is money.

In my decision-making process, I am willing to take on short-term debt for the opportunity of substantial recurring revenues; however, the lender requires collateral—collateral is what you pledge as a guarantee if the loan fails. So you can see why I am so against interest-only home mortgages. If you have no equity, it is not possible to get a Home Equity Line of Credit (HELOC).

The point of this is to build equity, whether it's in your home, your business, your property, or another venture. Equity is critical in reducing debt and building wealth. I've used a home equity line of credit with success once and commercial equity lines of credit on numerous occasions. This is another area for you to discuss with your trusted financial advisor. It's critical that you select the proper person to be a compass on credit lines and other issues that can impact your bottom line. Trust the Diva on this.

THE DIVA'S ADVICE

1. Avoid bad debt. There's no reading between the lines on this one. Avoid it. It works against your creating wealth.

2. Don't make reckless financial decisions. You may get away with it when you're twelve and buy something you shouldn't. When you're an adult and making long-term financial decisions, the stakes are too high for anything but reasonable risk. Consult your trusted financial advisor.

3. Do not contribute to your 401(k) account if you have outstanding credit card debt. Use that money to first pay off the credit cards. The interest rates on credit cards drain too much money from you. You are digging a bottomless pit.

4. Thinking about investing your home equity in the market? Think really carefully about it. Don't do it. Talk this over with an advisor as well.

5. There is good debt and bad debt. Knowing the difference is vital for your financial future.

6. Know how credit lines can help you increase equity and therefore wealth.

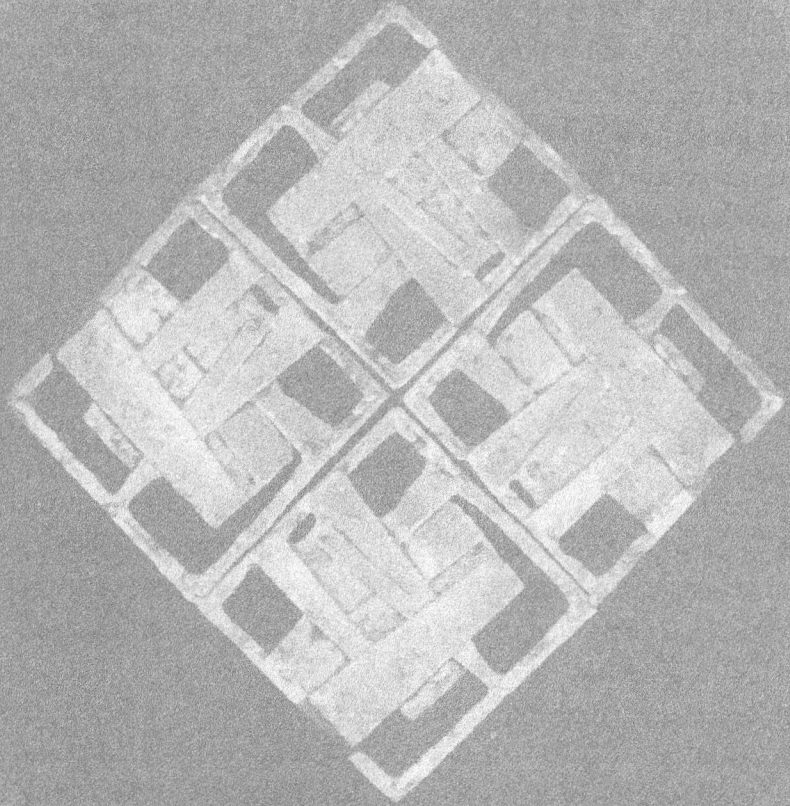

CHAPTER 11

Children and $Money

It's not what you earn, it's what you keep.
—Diva

Parents, children, and money are a bad mix. We have a huge problem in America. When it comes to good, old fashioned dollar sense, we cripple our children. We do it for the right reason: because we love them; however, our actions can often hinder our children's ability to learn to manage their own money. We have our reasons for our behavior: we want them to have everything we did not have; we want them to have it easier than we had it. What I have learned over the last twenty years is that this is a serious problem. We have crippled and enabled our children by giving them too much, too freely, and too often. And oftentimes, this is all done in the name of love!

A Young Lady with a Lot to Learn

Toby was beautiful and nineteen when she came to work for me. She had practically no handle on money. I know her parents very well. They are very successful and had given their children everything. Six months after coming to work for me, Toby was in my office when the subject of a car insurance premium payment came up. "You mean you pay this?" she asked. I told her I bought the car and paid for the insurance. I asked if she did the same for her expensive truck. Not only did she not pay for her truck; she didn't pay for her nails, hair care, or apartment. I asked her who was picking up the tab. Toby said, "I don't know. I just sign my name."

I had lunch with her father whom I like and respect very much, and during our conversation speculated that Toby would never find a husband to support her in such a lifestyle, particularly the young man she was dating.

A week later, Toby came to me and asked if I would show her how to open a checking account. I was shocked. Here was a young college student who had little understanding of money. It's no wonder some kids can't even make change at McDonald's.

Then there are children whose parents give them brand new cars or new toys simply because the children look like they want something. These children do not have any idea of the work involved in obtaining the money to pay for such gifts or how to manage their own income.

Uncle Sam is Everyone's Partner

One of my favorite all-time commercials is a McDonald's ad. The young man gets his first job, and he plans to take his family out to dinner with his first paycheck. You see him gleefully receiving his paycheck! He opens the check, and with astonishment on his face, he says, "Who is FICA and what is he doing with my money!" Next, you see the family dining at McDonald's. The point of the ad was that even if you don't make a lot of money, you can still take your family to McDonald's. However, there were other lessons as well.

The first lesson children need to learn is that it's not what you earn; it's what you keep. Just because you're being paid $400, doesn't mean your "take home" is actually $400. Generally speaking, most kids have no concept of how money works. The ad also proves another point adults and young adults both need to remember; everyone has at least one partner: Uncle Sam.

Children and Portfolios

During a client's self-discovery and disclosure process, we as financial advisors ask many, many questions to get a clear picture of your financial situation, including your risk tolerance.

As of recent years, I no longer ask, "Are you supporting any of your grown children?" Rather, I am compelled to ask, "How many of your grown children are you supporting?" On many occasions, I have heard the same story. Parents are embarrassed about the fact their children are not self-sufficient. The parents just don't know how to say no to their children. It's just easier to say yes and purchase the item the children want than to teach them the value of money.

It may be easier in the short term to just give in to the children, however in the long run, it does a terrible disservice to them. Now, thanks to their financial advisor, these parents can have a new answer. If you're in this situation, you should use it too. When you are asked for a non-necessity by your adult child who has mismanaged his or her money, you have the Diva's permission to say, "Well, let me see. I'll call my Financial Advisor and see if I have any money available."

The answer will always be "NO," unless you really want to give that child those funds. This allows you as a parent who loves your children and just cannot say "No" a way not to be the bad guy. I don't mind being the bad guy. The reason is that I have gone through this myself and I know it's hard; however, it is in the best interest of your children. We want them to be responsible adults, take care of their family, and give back to their community. For those of you who have children, nieces, nephews, or grandchildren, I'm going to give you some practical, usable advice. Even if you've wrecked your own children, you can still redeem yourself by teaching your grandchildren or anyone else you choose how to manage money. Remember, managing money is the one and only commonality we all share every day of our lives.

One final note: grown children should discuss financial plans with their parents when they reach their early 60s. They should know the location of their personal records and who their advisors are. They also need to know about their parents' living expenses and their insurance needs. It's wise to have up-to-date estate planning documents as well as knowing their parents' preferences for the future.

Lifelong Lessons

Since they were three years old, my nieces have had the opportunity to visit my husband and me every year as if we were their grandparents. No matter what's going on in the world or how busy everything is, we give them the opportunity to come visit. I have even taken them with me on business appointments when necessary.

I want to be the aunt who spoils them rotten and then gives them back to their parents to fix. However, I learned early on that not only did I get to spoil them and bond with them, it was also an opportunity to teach them life lessons that they were not going to learn elsewhere—especially not from their parents. My brother, Bo, and I are especially close, and he confesses, "I just can't help it. I want to give my kids everything we didn't have." So when the opportunity presented itself, I would take the time to teach them about money. Taylor, my brother's youngest, is the biggest challenge. She is a consumer and loves to shop and buy anything and everything! Our economy loves her.

When my nieces visit, we have a tradition that as soon as they come, we sit down and talk about household rules and how we treat one another, and why we have rules. There are only three rules, and sometimes they make up their own. They have to answer the question: "Why do we have rules?" The answer is, "So nobody gets in trouble, and we can spend our time together having fun." After the rules ceremony, our other tradition is to go to the grocery store and shop for food to make their favorite meals—everybody gets a night.

One of my nieces, Skylar, who was five-and-a-half, came by herself to stay with us for four or five days, so off we went to the local Albertsons. Eye level to this beautiful blue-eyed beauty of a niece was an Angelica doll. Of course, Skylar had to have her. She looked up at me with her big blue eyes and told me how much she had to have this doll. I seized on this opportunity to teach her about money as well as earning, managing, taxes, and giving. Despite the fact I really wanted to just have fun, I looked down at her and said, "Well, Skylar, where's your money?" She slapped both hands on her little blue jean shorts with her gingham ruffled shirt and sandals and said, "Aunt Bebe, I don't have any money!"

"So how are you gonna buy the doll, Skylar?"

Well, naturally she said, "You could buy it."

"Yes, I could; however, you see, I don't want the Angelica doll." She then took the doll off the shelf and held it next to her little angelic face and her bright red lips. She looked up at me and said, "But I need her!" How could I resist? Still, I stayed strong.

So I said, "Would you like me to show you how you can earn money to buy Angelica and then I will bring you back to the store to buy her?"

Now children do not trust you when you ask them this, even though you only lie to them about things that will bring them great joy, such as there is a Santa Claus, the Easter Bunny, Tooth Fairy. However, she considered this for a moment and asked, "Do you promise? Do you really promise you will bring me back?"

I said, "You earn the money, and I promise you I'll bring you back."

So we put Angelica back on the shelf and left the store hand in hand. My only fear was that they would be sold out by the time I took her back, yet it was a risk I was willing to take.

After returning home and unloading groceries, we sat on the sofa in the den and discussed how she could earn money. I patiently waited for the five-year-old to come up with ideas. I came up with things like doing the dishes or cleaning. She yelled, "Stop, stop, stop! I can't do anything inside; however, I can do anything outside." But then she stopped and said, "Well, what if I make my bed?"

"No, you have to make your bed anyway. We sleep in it, and we must make it up."

"How about brushing my teeth?"

"No, we have to brush our teeth every day."

So then, with her little hands placed on the back of the sofa, resting her little face on them while gazing out the window to the backyard (I'm being a very patient aunt here, by the way, and this doesn't happen that quickly.), she said, "Well, those flowers need to be watered out there."

I said, "Well, yes they do!"

"And ya know, Winston (our brown-eyed, black Shih Tzu) needs to be taken for a walk."

"Yes, he does!"

"And Winston needs a bath."

"Yes, he does."

By letting Skylar come up with the ideas on her own, she was more likely to do the jobs and meet her goals. All we care about here is success! Children are more likely to be enthusiastic about the jobs if you let them come up with them rather than just giving them the ideas.

Next, you must write down the job they're going to do as well as what you're going to pay them for these jobs. On a piece of paper, we had Skylar's goal—the Ms. Angelica Doll, what she could do to earn money, and how much she would earn. And it's very important to put this on the refrigerator! Kids love things on the refrigerator so they can see them. So she got up the next morning and saw on the refrigerator her list of things to do.

Now, when a child waters the plants, washes the dog, and walks the dog, keep in mind that the flowers are not going to be watered like you want them to be. In fact, they may be drowned, or they may just be sprinkled. The dog still may have soap on him when she's finished washing him. The point here is that you're teaching a lesson, a lifelong lesson, so get over the fact it is not done the way you would want. By the way, if you feel the dog wasn't cleaned properly, rinse the dog after the child goes to bed.

As the children complete each of their jobs, it's important to have the money ready and available. Don't just tell them you're going to give it to them; show them the money, Honey! Show them in one-dollar bills and give them an envelope to put their money in as they complete each job and put the envelope back on the refrigerator.

When Skylar completed her jobs and the weekend was almost over, it was time to count her money to be sure she had enough to pay for her Angelica doll. You can only imagine the surprise on her face when ten percent of that money was set aside on the kitchen table to go to charity—to give to someone, some church, some charity, or some other thing. Then she was even more surprised when we had to take another 10 percent of her money to put into savings, which meant another envelope. And then what was left over, she got to spend. Did I have to throw in an extra dollar for taxes so that she was covered? Of course I did. Remember this was a short weekend. She actually had to do another job to have enough money before I covered her.

When we were ready, she took her little envelope, we went to the store, walked in, and picked up Angelica, who had been waiting patiently for us. Remember, this was her money! Proudly cradling Angelica in her arms, she walked through the store and could barely see the cashier over the counter.

She looked at the lady, looked at Aunt Bebe (that's me), looked again at the cashier, and with both hands, gave her the envelope, and stated with all the confidence in the world, "I earned this myself" in the sweetest little southern drawl you've ever heard. The cashier and I both nearly burst into tears. The moment was priceless!

Remember, look for the opportunity. It will actually present itself. Allow your children to participate in deciding the jobs they're going to do. Help only if necessary. Write the goal, the jobs they're going to do, and what they're going to get paid for those jobs. Then put it on the refrigerator.

Pay them immediately for their work in one-dollar bills, no exceptions, no excuses. Give them their envelope to put the money in—it is now their possession—and put it back on the refrigerator. Finally, we must show them how they first should give, then they should save, and what's left over, they spend. It's all visually powerful.

Now repeat step one the next time they really, really, really want something.

Our School System Has Crippled Our Children!

Our education system has done a huge disservice to our children. Why? Because once students graduate, many don't know how to balance a checkbook, the pitfalls of credit card debt, the difference between a fifteen-year mortgage and a thirty-year mortgage, or how to purchase a vehicle. To make matters worse, far too many often cannot even make change at the store. As far as they're concerned, compounded interest is the eighth wonder of the world.

There is only *one* thing that we all have in common universally: if we choose to live on planet Earth, we will all manage money every single day of our lives! The only difference is how many zeros are at the end. It matters not your profession. You can be the president, a firefighter, a truck driver, a teacher, a homemaker, Bill Gates, Donald Trump, or Oprah Winfrey. Whatever the case, you must have the basics of managing money in order to be the best provider for yourself, your family, your children's education, your charitable organizations, and community as well as your retirement plan.

The basics are simply these: we're spending it, saving it, or investing it; and mostly, we're spending it at a greater rate than we are earning it. This is an urgent crisis!

I personally invest my time and resources to support Financial Literacy Legislation in Oklahoma. Naturally, I feel frustrated that anything of this importance should take this long. It is appalling to me that we still don't have mandatory financial management in our school systems as a requirement for graduation. The Oklahoma Society of Certified Public Accountants, the Oklahoma Bankers

Association, and the Oklahoma Department of Securities have all recognized this need. They provide educational materials, programs, and/or websites because they know the statistics, and they know the need is there; yet classes for financial management are still not required in Oklahoma Schools.

The debate within the State Legislature is what course curriculum should we use, how many hours/semesters are needed, what courses do we eliminate, and at what grade do we start? 'Blah, Blah, Blah,' is what I have to say about that. There are already great curriculums out there that have been created, are available, and are being used across the country on a limited basis. I have personally met some of the instructors teaching these courses. So this debate is a waste of time! No courses have to be eliminated. I don't care if it's put in physical education, home room, social studies, or math. Just give the information somewhere during the course of the day!

The debate about semesters, hours, and what grade to start doesn't fly either. I have taught five-year-olds (Skylar) how to properly give, save, and spend. I have been the selected speaker for a Sophomore Leadership Program sponsored by Arvest Bank to share the pitfalls of credit card debt and how easy it can be to become a millionaire. I know how powerful sharing this knowledge can be. Recently, a father approached me at a business event introduced himself and wanted to thank me—for what I am not sure. Clearly, I had never met this man. You see, his son was in one of these Leadership Programs, and the father wanted to thank me and share with me the impact the knowledge I shared made on his son's life! Was it time well invested? I think so.

That was only a thirty-minute introduction to the basics of financial literacy. Just think what could be accomplished if we started at a younger age and with more consistency!

It is our responsibility to give our children the tools to succeed in this fast-paced global economy, and we are failing miserably. I call on every State Education Department to do the right thing for our children and DO IT NOW!

THE DIVA'S ADVICE

1. We are raising a generation of young people almost financially illiterate. Some are in college and can't balance a checkbook. Parents say they buy almost everything for their offspring because they love them. If you truly love a child, teach them the real value of money.

2. One of the first lessons all children need to learn about money is Uncle Sam is everyone's partner. Most adults need to remember that as well.

3. Married, grown-up children can have a profound effect on their parents' portfolio. Some parents never learn to say "no" to their adult children. Parents need to remember two valuable words: "tough love."

4. Grown children should discuss financial plans with their parents when they reach their early 60s.

5. A child is almost never too young to learn about the true value of money.

6. Having a child learn the value of setting a goal and working and earning their way will pay dividends throughout their life.

7. Our educational system has failed our youngsters as well. All school systems need to teach money basics.

66

When it comes to good, old fashioned dollar sense, we cripple our children. We do it for the right reason: because we love them; however, our actions can often hinder our children's ability to learn to manage their own money.

99

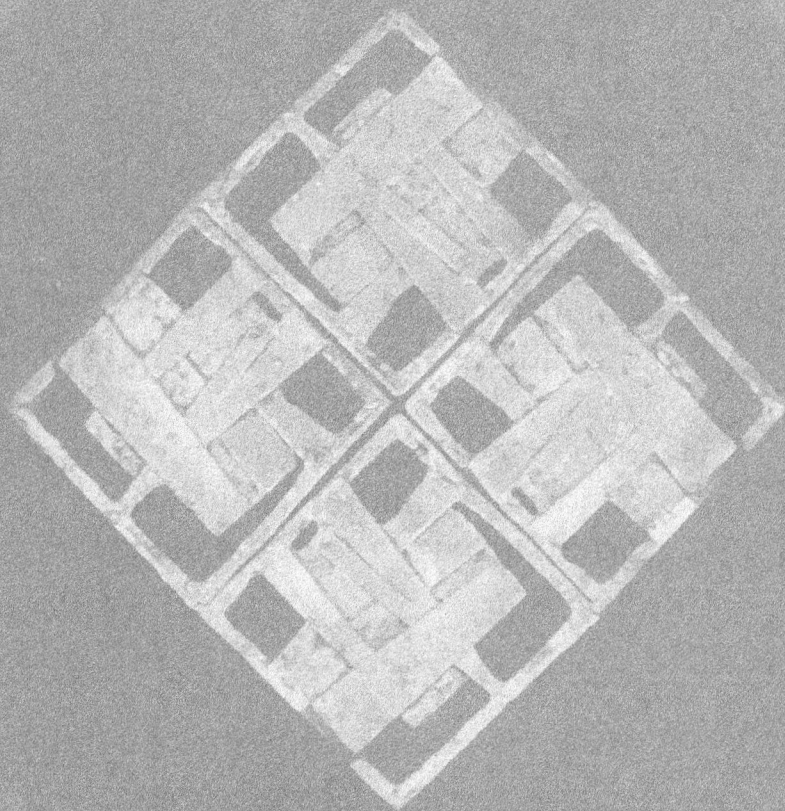

CHAPTER 12

The Decision is Yours

It's not where you start, it's where you finish.
—Diva

W hat stage of life are you at? Are you interested in a secure retirement or perhaps setting up a college fund? Are you interested in the peace of mind a sound financial future can provide? Perhaps you're unsure of investments or real estate opportunities. Maybe you just want to make sure you make the most informed financial decisions possible. If for no other reason, it's your money.

In any of the above cases, it's important to find the right advisor and know that it must be a partnership. If you don't get that sense of partnership from your advisor, then it's time to end that relationship and find someone you can trust.

Remember, there is a huge difference between having a financial advisor and having someone who sells you the latest product from the corporate office. Don't select this person casually. Ask the right questions (See Chapter 4).

Make sure the advisor is willing to return calls and cares directly about you. I cannot emphasize this enough. A lot of our business may appear to be charts, figures, and facts; that's just a part of the story. The most important detail of any venture is the human element. As I've said in this book from almost the beginning, one size doesn't fit all. This most certainly applies to the people who sit across from me at the table. They are the most important part of the equation. My clients, those at my speeches, or those listening to my radio show have their own dreams, aspirations, and yearning for their future and the future of their loved ones. This cannot be underestimated.

Knowledge Is Power

What you do with your portfolio will have a lasting impact well into retirement and for the legacy of your heirs. In addition to money and assets, you can leave your heirs something even more powerful: good common sense when it comes to dealing with finances. Teach them about avoiding bad credit. Teach them about good credit. And, while you're at it, brush up on the lessons yourself.

There is so much to know when planning a future for you and your money. It is a minefield out there. Hopefully, our little journey here has given you the ability to be on the lookout for some of the red flags when making monetary decisions.

All of us have made mistakes with our treasure. Chalk it up to the collective experience known as life. Your financial advisor is there to make sure those little learning ventures are kept to a minimum. Don't forget the story of the man and his baseball card business. I fear he most likely did dip into his $500,000 401(k) account to finance this risky idea. This was despite my warnings. Had he left that account alone, it most likely would be soaring well past the $1 million mark for his retirement. His life lesson probably cost him at least $1 million. That's just the dollar value. How much did it most likely cost him in frustration? Peace of mind? And the most important treasure of all: time?

Know when it's wise to act. I could have sold my former bank building to a developer when its value wasn't much more than what I had originally paid for it. Instead, I waited. I didn't wait until the property had no value; I sold it when it was of the most value to the developer. In thirty-six months, the price of the property went from my initial $110,000 investment to almost $1 million. The timing was right, and the proper financial advisor can help you know when the timing is right for you.

A Quick Review

Let's review some of the areas where a financial advisor can make a difference.

- Determining where you are and putting together a net worth statement.
- Helping you set financial goals.
- Providing real estate advice, whether it's what to look for on closing day or if a reverse mortgage is a good idea for you.
- Putting you on the right path to a prosperous and happy retirement.
- Helping you stay out of debt.
- Steering you in the direction of good debt, which grows businesses and enhances your wealth.
- Making sound decisions for you and your heirs on inheritance.
- Knowing the difference between a solid investment and sheer folly.
- Tax efficiency.

Your advisor can be the go between with you and your banker as well as attorney and CPA. Remember, owner Jerry Jones of the Dallas Cowboys can purchase some of the finest football talent in the universe. He can hire the right marketing team and stadium personnel to put on a first-class game. What's Jerry missing? Without a good coach, he can never get the most from the team on the field. Without a top-notch team, the work of his marketing crew and stadium personnel is for nothing.

That's the same with you and your financial advisor. The advisor, your monetary partner, will work with the various entities to make sure your asset ledger is in the finest shape possible. Your financial advisor should be working as the symphony conductor leading the orchestra, and you both need to be making beautiful money music together.

The Decisions Are up to You

I have enjoyed showing you how it's your money, Honey! And the best ways to enhance and protect it. Yet from my days in Texas, I can't help but think of the old saying, "You can lead a horse to water, but you can't make him drink." I assume my clients and most of my readers and radio listeners will be smart enough to drink.

Since you've been wise enough to purchase this book and follow me to this point, I know you have the commitment and desire to succeed. Your time is a valuable investment, and I salute you for being wise enough to recognize this and show the desire to improve yourself. In chapter four, I made a few points worth revisiting. First, I can't select the person to be your most trusted financial advisor. That is your decision. We've provided guidelines and the questions for you to ask. Remember the questions to ask potential candidates, and don't be shy. Write them down. Your potential advisors won't mind your bringing the list. If they do, keep looking.

Second, I've included a glossary of terms used frequently in this industry. Please, familiarize yourself with them. Know about reverse mortgages. Know about rebalancing. What you don't know can hurt you and your money.

I can't tell you how honored I am to have shared this reading journey with you. Don't be hesitant about going back over a lot of the information we've covered. I like to use a yellow highlighter when I come across a point in a book I've read. If you feel too guilty about marking up this book, just buy another!

While you're at it, don't stop with what you've learned here. This experience is only the beginning. This applies not only to you, it applies to me as well. When faced with a minefield, get all the facts and information on your side. Believe me, it can never hurt.

Yet, one final word of caution: America and much of the western industrialized world have been blessed by offering their people an abundant set of opportunities. Knowledge and timing can lead you to the opportunities that are right for you. Please never let greed cloud your thinking. When preparing for a key decision, a level head armed with facts is the best approach. Be sure to get together with your advisor before leaping.

After the glossary, I have included my own personal reading list. It ranges from King Solomon's eternal advice from Proverbs to the valuable nuggets of knowledge from Dr. Joseph Murphy's *The Power of Your Subconscious Mind*. I strongly urge you to read as many of these books as you can. Your mind is the most valuable asset God has given you. Please, invest in it.

Finally, your financial future relies on other hard work. The nuts and bolts of your personal portfolio will rely on some key information you must gather for both yourself and your advisor.

Please, log onto FinancialDiva.com. Download the simple Net Worth, Budget, and Financial Goal forms, and get started or update your financial plan today. In order to ascertain where you want to go with your financial plans, you need to know where you are and where you've been. Write down your goals and keep revisiting them.

THE DIVA'S ADVICE

1. Working with your trusted financial advisor is crucial. The advisor is one of the most important partners you'll have in life.
2. When it comes to finances, knowledge is power.
3. We've all made mistakes. We can learn from them. Your advisor can help make sure your blunders aren't too costly.
4. There are so many areas where a trusted advisor can help you. Your advisor brings together many parties to make your financial future sound.
5. Continue your financial education. Read other books and review this one often.
6. Look for reasons to get things done. Start a plan today.
7. Your future is in your hands. Make it the best you can!

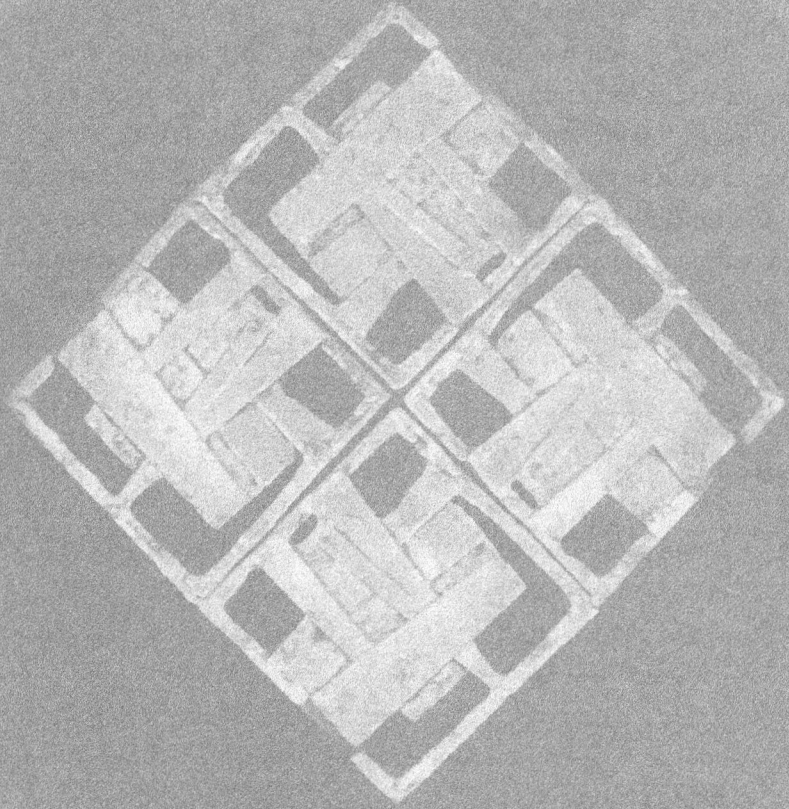

Formulate a Plan!

Your financial future is in your hands. You can make the wise choices. Your life is your No. 1 investment. For your sake and the sake of your loved ones, make your life a happy one, because after all, It's *All* About The $Money, Honey!® May God bless you always!

Closing Thought
The best advice I can give you: don't take advice from broke people.
—Diva

HOW WE DO IT

Our Unique Process

Through our unique six-step process, we listen to what's causing you pain and seek to understand your goals and dreams. From there, we recommend and implement customized strategies to meet your needs.

1. Initial Strategy Review
2. Discovery of Your Goals
3. Customized Recommendations
4. Implementation
5. Delivery of Financial Organizer
6. Monitoring and Reporting

Universe of Solutions

Our advisors are fiduciaries required to work on behalf of your best interests. We use a team approach, engaging the best wealth management professionals and strategists the industry has to offer, working in tandem with your CPA and Trust Attorney to build your customized plan.

- Open Architecture Platform
- Domestic/International Partners
- 2,000 Global Researchers
- Investments and Insurance
- Social Investing
- Donor Advised Funds

Client Service

- Quarterly Market Update Letter
- Strategy Reviews
- Portfolio Monitoring
- E-Newsletters
- Exclusive Client Events
- Family Meetings

Implementing your customized strategies is only the beginning. Our service and communication afterward truly set us apart. Keeping you in the know on key news and issues affecting your family's financial well-being is what has led ChappelWood to maintaining 98 percent of its clients.

Compelling Technology

- Online Account Access
- Risk Speed Limit Analysis
- Custom Portfolio Analysis
- Custom Income Planning Tools
- Online Resources
- Webinars, Podcasts, and Videos

Above all, we want to build a personal relationship with you. Yet, we also understand you want access to the best technology when it comes to your financial plan. We make a significant investment in the most compelling technology our industry can provide to enhance your experience with us.

We use a team approach, engaging the best wealth management professionals and strategists the industry has to offer, working in tandem with your CPA and Trust Attorney to build your customized plan.

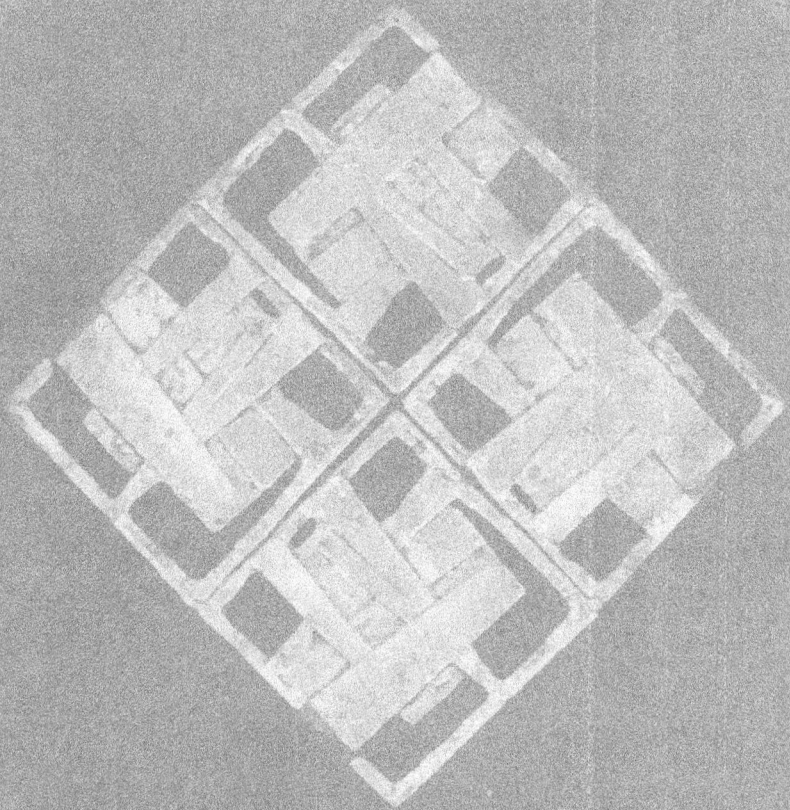

Glossary of Valuable Financial Terms

401(k): This qualified retirement plan allows eligible employees to contribute a certain amount of compensation on a pre-tax basis; earnings are tax deferred. Employers may match a stated percentage of employee contributions to the plan. In many cases, employees have general responsibilities for investment choices and enjoy the direct tax savings. The reduced cost and liability of 401(k) plans appeal to many employers.

403(b): Similar to the 401(k), this type of qualified retirement plan is available to employees of nonprofit and government organizations.

Annuity: This long-term contract sold by life insurance companies guarantees payments (based on the claims-paying ability of the issuing insurer), fixed or variable, to the purchaser at regular intervals. Fixed annuities offer consistent, predictable returns, whereas variable annuities provide fluctuating returns based on the performance of an investment portfolio. Payments are usually scheduled to begin at a future time, such as retirement. In certain cases, payment may begin immediately. Some annuities provide tax-deferred earnings, often as part of retirement plans.

Annuity Payout Option: Payments from an annuity may be received in a variety of ways: as a fixed dollar amount, for a fixed period, or over the lifetime(s) of one or two annuitants. The annuitant chooses one of these alternatives as the payout option.

Asset: An asset is any property with a cash value that is expected to provide future benefit, such as real estate, equipment, savings, and investments.

Asset Allocation: This process divides investments among different asset classes, such as stocks, bonds, and cash. The goal of asset allocation is to reduce portfolio risk through diversification.

Asset Class: An asset class is a specific category of assets or investments, such as cash, bonds, stocks, or real estate. Assets in the same category tend to share similar characteristics and behave similarly in the marketplace.

Bear Market: A bear market is characterized by an extended period of declining prices, usually by 20 percent, in the financial markets. A prolonged downturn of general economic activity is often the catalyst for a bear market in stocks, whereas rising interest rates are typically responsible for a bear market in bonds. The bear market is the opposite of a bull market.

Beta: A beta is a measure of a security's price fluctuations (volatility) relative to an appropriate market index. For example, the Standard & Poor's 500 Stock Index (S&P 500) has a beta of one. Stocks with betas greater than one are subject to more rapid and extreme price fluctuations than the market. Conversely, price fluctuations for stocks with betas less than one are less frequent and smaller than the market. Conservative investors generally seek securities with lower beta values, while aggressive investors seek those with higher beta values.

Bond: This debt security issued by a corporation, government, or governmental agency obligates the issuer to pay interest at predetermined intervals and repay the principal at maturity. Every bond has a set face value, also known as a par value, which names the amount of money the bondholder will receive when the bond reaches the date of maturity. The face value will never change, while the market value of a bond may fluctuate. If a bondholder sells a bond before its date of maturity, he or she may receive more or less than the face value.

Broker: This financial professional mediates between the buyer and seller during the trading of services or property, such as securities, real estate, insurance, or commodities. In return for services, the broker generally receives a commission.

Budget: Projected income and expenses for a given period is called a budget. A surplus budget indicates profits are expected; a balanced budget anticipates that revenues will equal expenses; and a deficit budget suggests expenses will exceed expenses.

Bull Market: A bull market is characterized by an extended period of rising security prices, usually by 20 percent in financial markets. A high volume of trading often occurs in a bull market, which is the opposite of a bear market.

Buy-and-Hold: This investment strategy advocates holding securities for the long term, while ignoring short-term price fluctuations in the market. Unlike market-timing investors, who actively buy and sell securities hoping to turn quick profits on short-term price fluctuations, investors who buy and hold securities hope for substantial gains over time.

Capital Gains Tax: This tax is levied on profits from the sale of securities or other assets, such as land, buildings, equipment, and furniture.

Commission: This fee is charged by an agent for his/her services in facilitating a transaction, such as buying or selling securities or real estate, based on the dollar amount of the trade, the transaction, or the number of shares involved.

Common Stock: This security represents partial ownership, also called equity, in a corporation. Common stock ownership entitles a shareholder to participate in stockholder meetings and to vote for the board of directors.

Compounding: This process applies investment growth not only to the original investment but also to income and gains reinvested in prior periods. To illustrate, if you earn compound interest on savings, you earn interest on the principal amount and the accumulated interest, as it is earned. If you earn simple interest on savings, you earn interest based only on the principal amount.

Coverdell Education Savings Account (Coverdell ESA): Formerly known as the Education IRA, this savings vehicle allows parents to accumulate tax-free savings on money earmarked for a child's college education. There are limits on income eligibility and on how much may be set aside per year.

Credit Line: This revolving agreement allows a person to borrow any amount up to a pre-approved limit for purchases or cash advances. As the outstanding balance is paid off, credit again becomes available to fund new purchases or cash advances.

Direct Rollover: A direct rollover is the tax-free transfer of money or property from the trustee or custodian of one qualified retirement plan or account to another.

Diversification: This investment strategy is designed to reduce the risk of investing in a single industry/market sector or a small number of companies by spreading the risk over several industries/market sectors or a larger number of companies. The operating assumption is that diversified investments are unlikely to all move in the same direction, allowing gains in one investment to offset the losses of another.

Dow Jones Industrial Average (DJIA): The Dow Jones Industrial Average is the price-weighted average of thirty actively traded blue chip stocks on the New York Stock Exchange (NYSE). The DJIA represents approximately 15 percent to 20 percent of the market value of NYSE stocks.

Early Withdrawal: An early withdrawal is the removal of funds from a fixed-rate investment before the maturity date or from a tax-deferred investment or retirement savings account before a pre-determined time. One example would be a distribution from an individual retirement account (IRA) taken before age fifty-nine-and-a-half. Early withdrawals may be subject to a penalty.

Equity: Equity can be defined as anything that represents ownership interests, such as stock in a company. Equity also generally refers to the difference between an asset's current market value and the debt against it. For example, if you own a car valued at $15,000, but owe $10,000 on a car loan, your equity in the car is $5,000.

Estate Planning: This process plans for the orderly administration and disposition of a person's assets after he or she dies.

Fiduciary: A fiduciary is an individual who provides investment advice for a fee or who exercises discretionary authority or control in managing assets. Also, a fiduciary can refer to an individual, company, or association responsible for holding assets in trusts and investing them wisely for the benefit of a trust's beneficiary. Examples or fiduciaries include trustees, bankruptcy receivers, and executors of wills and estates.

Fixed Annuity: A fixed annuity is an investment contract sold by a life insurance company that guarantees regular payments to the purchaser for a specified period of time, or for life. The purchaser generally pays a premium either in a lump sum or in installments.

Gift Tax: This tax is levied by the federal government, and some states, on assets transferred from one person to another. The tax rate increases with the value of the gift. The donor pays the tax, not the recipient.

Index: An index is a hypothetical portfolio of securities that represents a particular market or portion of it. Indexes are used to measure the amount of change in a particular security by comparing it to the change of similar companies. Some well-known indexes are the New York Stock Exchange Index (NYSE), the American Stock Exchange Index (AMEX), the Standard & Poor's 500 Index (S&P 500), the Russell 2000 Index, and the Value Line Index.

Individual Retirement Account (IRA): An IRA is a tax-deferred retirement savings account that allows individuals to contribute a limited amount per year. A traditional IRA may allow individuals, depending on their incomes and participation in employer-sponsored retirement plans, to deduct part or all of their contributions on their tax returns. Withdrawals made after age fifty-nine-and-a-half are taxed at the current tax rate. In contrast, Roth IRAs allow individuals to withdraw earnings tax free, provided they have owned the account for five years and are at least age fifty-nine-and-a-half. Contributions are made with after-tax dollars.

Inflation: Inflation is the general rise in the price level of goods and services that occurs when demand increases relative to supply. Inflation is usually measured by the Consumer Price Index (CPI) and the Producer Price Index (PPI). As a result of inflation, the purchasing power of the dollar decreases. For example, if inflation occurs at 3 percent annually, $100 in one year would be worth only $97 in the next.

Lexicon: The particular vocabulary associated with a profession, activity, or field of interest.

Like-Kind Exchange: A transaction under United States law that specifies that if an asset (usually some form of real estate such as land or a building) is sold and the proceeds of the sale are then reinvested in a like-kind asset, then no gain or loss is recognized, allowing the deferment of capital gains taxes that would otherwise have been due on the first sale. This law is defined by section 1031 of the Internal Revenue Code 26 (U.S.C. 1031).

Like-Kind Exchanges (Real Estate Tax Tips): Generally, if you exchange business or investment property solely for business or investment property of a like-kind, no gain or loss is recognized under Internal Revenue Code Section 1031. If, as part of the exchange, you also receive other (not like-kind) property or money, gain is recognized to the extent of the other property and money received, but a loss is not recognized.

Like-Kind Property: Properties are of like-kind, if they are of the same nature or character, even when they differ in grade or quality. Personal properties of a like class are like-kind properties; however, livestock of different sexes are not like-kind properties. Also, personal property used predominantly in the United States and personal property used predominantly outside the United States are not like-kind properties.

Living Trust: Also called an inter vivos trust, a living trust is established by a living person and allows that person to control the assets he or she contributes to the trust.

Market Risk: Also called systematic risk, market risk is the portion of a security's risk common to all securities in the same asset class, and it cannot be eliminated through diversification. For example, a market risk associated with investment in stocks is the general tendency of share prices to decrease during an economic downturn.

Millionaire: A person worth a million, or millions, of dollars.

National Association of Securities Dealers Automated Quotations (NASDAQ): NASDAQ is a computerized system that facilitates trading and provides current price quotes for the most actively traded over-the-counter (OTC) securities.

Net Worth: The amount of asset value exceeding total liabilities is referred to as net worth.

New York Stock Exchange (NYSE): Also called The Big Board and The Exchange, the NYSE is the oldest and largest stock exchange in the U.S., listing the country's largest corporations. Memberships are sold to brokers, who buy and sell stocks on the floor of the exchange.

Portfolio: A portfolio is the combined security holdings of an individual investor or mutual fund. The objective of holding investments in a portfolio is to reduce risk through diversification.

Qualified Plan: A qualified plan is a retirement plan that meets the requirements of Section 401(a) of the Internal Revenue Code; one that is, therefore, eligible for tax-favored treatment.

Rebalancing: Over time, market conditions and the varied performance of asset classes may cause the portfolio's asset mix to vary from the original target allocation. To remain consistent with the asset allocation guidelines established, each asset class shall be reviewed periodically, typically quarterly, to maintain the initial target allocation.

Required Minimum Distribution (RMD): The RMD is the legally required minimum annual amount that must be distributed from a retirement account to an IRA holder or qualified plan participant. RMDs, which are calculated by dividing the year-end account balance by the applicable distribution period or life expectancy, must begin by April 1 of the year following the year the individual reaches the Required Minimum Distribution (RMD) age of seventy-two.

Reverse Mortgage: This type of loan is used to turn home equity into cash. The lender makes regular tax-free payments or a lump sum payment to the homeowner (borrower), which are usually used to fund retirement needs.

Risk Tolerance: Risk tolerance is the measurement of an investor's willingness or ability to handle declines in the value of his or her investment portfolio. For many investors, risk tolerance is an important consideration when developing a diversification strategy for a portfolio.

Rollover: A rollover is a tax-free transfer of funds from one retirement plan to another.

Roth IRA: A Roth IRA is a type of Individual Retirement Account (IRA) in which contributions are nondeductible. Earnings grow tax deferred, and distributions are tax free, provided you have owned the account for five years and are at least age fifty-nine-and-a-half.

Securities and Exchange Commission (SEC): The SEC is the primary federal regulatory agency for the securities industry, whose responsibility is to promote full public disclosure and protect investors against fraudulent and manipulative practices. In addition to regulation and protection, it also monitors corporate takeovers in the U.S. The SEC is composed of five commissioners appointed by the president and approved by the senate.

Self-Directed IRA (SDIRA): A self-directed IRA is an individual retirement arrangement that allows a holder a wider choice of investments, including stocks, bonds, mutual funds, and money market funds. SDIRAs may be opened at institutions with trust powers, state FDIC-insured institutions, federal credit unions, and federally chartered savings banks or savings and loans.

Standard & Poor's 500 Index (S&P 500): The S&P 500 is an index of 500 of the most widely held common stocks on the New York Stock Exchange (NYSE). It is used as a measure to indicate the overall health of the U.S. stock market.

Stock: A stock is a security representing partial ownership, also called equity, in a corporation. Each stock share represents a proportionate claim against the company's profits and assets. Common stock entitles shareholders to participate in stockholder meetings and to vote for the board of directors. Preferred stock does not confer voting rights, yet it takes precedence in claims against profits and assets.

Stock Market: The stock market is a general term referring to the organized trading of securities in the various market exchanges and the over-the-counter (OTC) market.

Strategic Asset Allocation Approach: The strategic asset allocation approach tends to maintain a more fixed asset mix throughout the investment time horizon. Based upon your risk/return parameters, the asset mix is determined by first deciding which asset classes to include in the portfolio, followed by an in-depth analysis of the characteristics of each asset class, including return, risk or volatility, and covariance (the diversification effect). Then an optimizer develops the optimum combination of these asset classes to meet your desired level of risk and return. Once the long-term asset mix has been established, the portfolio is rebalanced periodically to maintain a constant level of risk exposure throughout the investment period.

Tactical Asset Allocation Approach: The tactical asset allocation approach also utilizes the principles of Modern Portfolio Theory to establish the long-term target asset mix for the portfolio. Unlike the strategic approach, however, tactical asset allocation establishes permissible ranges for each of the asset classes. Investment analysts then gather current market research in an effort to make judgments as to the relative attractiveness of each asset class at a given moment in time. Then the asset mix in the portfolio is adjusted to overweight or underweight specific asset classes to reflect changing global capital market conditions. The ultimate goal of tactical asset allocation is to improve the risk-adjusted return in the overall strategy by accurately recognizing changing investment opportunities.

Time Horizon: The time horizon is the projected length of time for which an investor plans to hold investments.

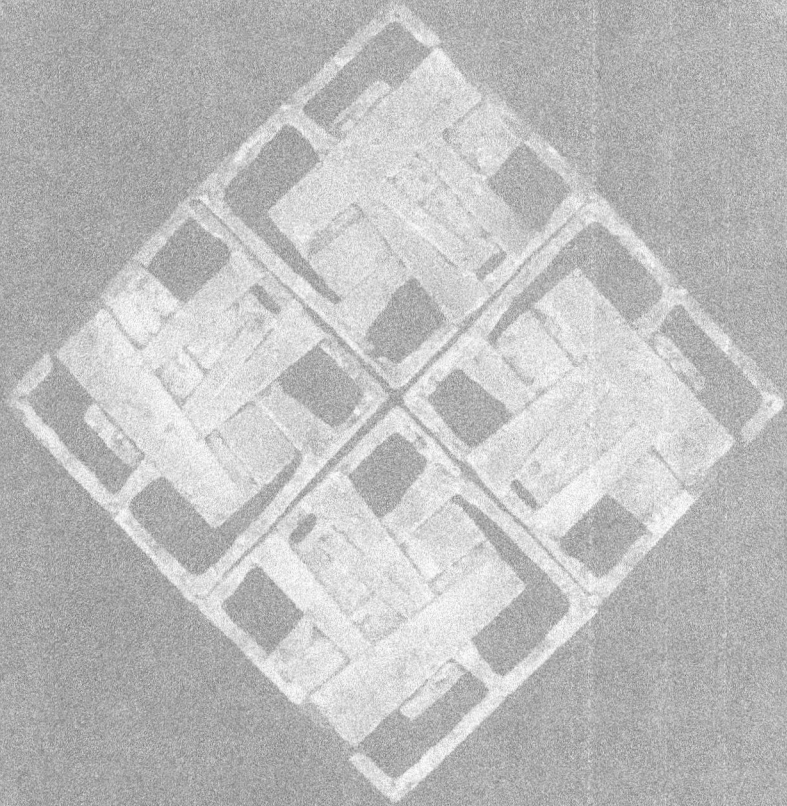

Reading List

These books are among my personal favorites! They are inspirational, educational, and informative. These are just a few of the thousands of books that I've read and enjoyed. You've got to start somewhere. Select one from the list below and start today!

- Allen, James. *As a Man Thinketh*
- Cardone, Grant *The 10X Rule*
- Cardone, Grant *Be Obsessed or Be Average*
- Cordes, Ronald, Brian O'Toole, and Richard Steiny. *The Art of Investing and Portfolio Management*
- The *Bible* (Proverbs in particular)
- Friedman, Thomas L. *The World is Flat: A Brief History of the Twenty-first Century*
- Hilton, Conrad N. *Be My Guest*
- J.W. Marriott, Jr. and Kathi Ann Brown *The Spirit to Serve Marriott's Way*
- Morris, Virginia B. and Kenneth Morris *A Woman's Guide to Investing*
- Murphy, Dr. Joseph. *The Power of Your Subconscious Mind*
- Muse, Lamar. *Southwest Passage: The Inside Story of Southwest Airlines' Formative Years*

- Robbins, Anthony. *Awaken the Giant Within*
- Stanley, Thomas J. and William D. Danko. *The Millionaire Next Door*
- Stein, Ben. *How Successful People Win*

Website
Recommendations

- FinancialDiva.com: know more about your author, the Financial Diva, Victoria L. Woods. Order a 50-page transcript and CD of *Humble Beginnings* or learn more about her guest speaker appearances.
- ChappelWood.com: financial calculators and financial glossary.
- investeedok.org: educational, objective information sponsored by Oklahoma Securities Commission and produced by the University of Oklahoma.

To Reach the Diva by Phone, Call:
1-888 838-DIVA (3482)

About the Author

Victoria Woods lives by the motto proudly displayed on a plaque in her office: "The one who says it cannot be done should never interrupt the one doing it."

Victoria has been the one "doing it" for many years now. Her vibrant personality and seemingly boundless energy are her trademarks, making her a favorite with the media. Victoria is founder, CEO, and Chief Investment Advisor to millionaires for ChappelWood Financial Services in Edmond, Oklahoma and has clients nationwide.

A successful entrepreneur and investor, Victoria mixes wit and wisdom as she shares practical, easy-to-understand advice on the world of finance in her books, speaking engagements, radio show, and through her website. She is a master when it comes to helping others maneuver the sometimes-tempestuous waters of investing.

With years of experience in sales, sales training, professional speaking, and business management, Victoria brings a unique perspective to all she undertakes. Her training, experience, and knowledge propelled her career to impressive heights, earning her numerous awards and honors.

Victoria was selected as a White House Conference Delegate and a member of the President's Advisory Board. She was also named the National Association of Women Business Owners "Best of the Best," and one of *The Journal Record's* 50 Most Influential Women.

Initially appointed by the governor as a commissioner and serving as finance chair, Victoria serves as the state chair for the Oklahoma Commission on the Status of Women.

In addition, Victoria founded Women for Financial Independence, an organization that helps women learn the strategies of investing and finance.

Visit FinancialDiva.com for information
about speaking engagements.

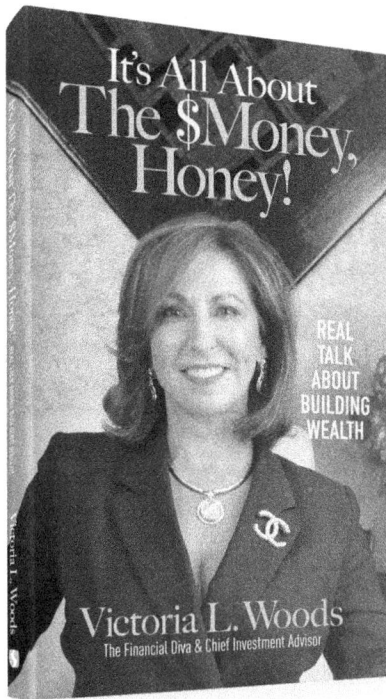

It's All About The $Money, Honey!

REAL TALK ABOUT BUILDING WEALTH

Victoria L. Woods
The Financial Diva & Chief Investment Advisor

Let's Engage!

f TheFinancialDiva

𝕏 FinancialDiva

▶ financialdiva

◉ financialdiva_

in financialdiva

FOR SPEAKING, WORKSHOP OPPORTUNITIES AND TO ORDER ADDITIONAL BOOKS OR BOOKS IN BULK (GREAT AS CLIENT GIFTS!) VISIT: FINANCIALDIVA.COM